Shannon -
Find your Still
and live a life of
peace !
love Dave

*This book is dedicated to seekers looking for answers, feelers
desiring higher emotional intelligence, and dreamers
committed to creating change in the world.*

"When there is no more separation between "this" and "that,"
it is called the still-point of the Tao. At the still point in the
center of the circle one can see the infinite in all things."
- Chuang-tzu

STILL POINT

INNER PEACE IS THE NEW SUCCESS

By Dave Lopez and Joey McCarthy

TABLE OF CONTENTS

Introduction

PART I. LIFE'S A FUNNY THING

PART II. THE 7 OBSTACLES TO PEACE

PART III. THE PATH TO STILLNESS

PART IV. A POWERFUL WORLD VIEW

Introduction

"We can never obtain peace in the outer world until we make peace with ourselves." - Dalai Lama

Hello Self

We'd all benefit from knowing ourselves just a bit better. To understand how we operate would make life easier and help navigate relationships more effortlessly. It would be so awesome if humans came with an operator's manual, but the problem is that we're not born into families in which those instructions arrive with birth. So how do we connect the dots without a guide? Through trial and error, we learn what works and what doesn't. We begin to see that which brings us joy and that which delivers misery. Friends and mentors provide us with direction and new ways of thinking. We learn to make sense of our feelings because they reveal our personal truths.

Obstacles to Inner Peace

It can be said that the greatest human goal is peace of mind. The greatest obstacle to peace of mind is our emotions run amok. Life is a series of experiences that trigger our emotions, and ultimately our actions. By understanding these feelings, we develop a deeper emotional intelligence. There are many examples of things we've done or said that we wish we would've done or said differently. Looking back, it's easy to see how many of our actions led us toward unwanted stress and anxiety. Recognizing the 7 Obstacles To Peace gives us ammunition to fight for self-actualization. We discover how to take better care of ourselves and in the process, achieve peace of mind.

Taking responsibility for our lives starts with taking responsibility for our emotions. Applying intelligence to them means thinking them through before acting. There's no reason to keep taking the same actions over again, if we're unhappy with the results. Something magical happens when we assume greater responsibility for our happiness. It places us in a position to become empowered, connected, and ignited. We can live without shackles, free and liberated. Living with a peaceful nature, we can invite experiences that we desire. We are no longer in response-mode to conditions and circumstances out of our control. Being calm, we can react to our emotions more intelligently.

We all face pain, turmoil and conflict. Just as we all face these things, we have the potential to change our relationship to them. A history of living life on other people's terms illustrates the void it can create in our own. Mastering our emotions means we can live with intention, self-reliance and commitment.

Something may not be working in our lives. It may be relationships, career, love-life, or it might just be our level of personal happiness. Whatever it is, we might not be reaching our potential. There are several reasons as to why this might be the case. When we realize that the here-and-now isn't satisfying, it is often the result of living from an unconscious nature. In this state, we experience victim status, knee-jerk reactions, and doing things the way they've always been done.

Naturally, this poses a threat to our happiness because outside circumstances ultimately control it.

A Different View

Those of us wanting to take control of our lives seek out tools and techniques to view things differently. We want the opportunity to create an environment of peace and serenity. In short, we desire self-mastery to deliver an improved quality of life and meaningful relationships.

In an era where people take offense so readily, it's important to recognize that a beneficial solution for handling difficulties is to go inward and master our own emotions. Until we do so, we are at the mercy of others or institutions to make us feel OK or happy. Taking offense has its roots in a strong ego identification. The journey of the soul is one in which we uncover the potential to connect with happiness and recognize that at some profound level, we have created our realities through our beliefs. What we believe and how we perceive things lays the foundation for our world views. Events that happen to us are fundamentally neutral and have no effect, except if we choose.

The choices we make reveal if we are truly committed to happiness. As our actions lead us in that direction, we connect with an inner calm that we might never have known. That Still Point is the base of our connectedness and our personal power. Embracing and activating love-conscious actions and eliminating fear-based actions leads us there.

The path to stillness is the most direct route to an empowered life and our responsibility is to connect with it wholly. A true measure of success includes an assessment of how we define it. Holding onto traditional views of success can actually cause anxiety and unhappiness. To have it all financially, but to lack peace of mind, is to be bankrupt. Inner peace is the new success.

Part I

Life's a Funny Thing

"It's a funny thing about life, if you refuse to accept anything but the best, you very often get it." - W. Somerset Maugham

CHAPTER 1

THE WAY LIFE WORKS

"Life is inherently risky. There is only one big risk you should avoid at all costs, and that is the risk of doing nothing."
- Denis Waitley

The Human Condition

We're a funny lot, us humans. We can see the best and worst in humanity on any given day and at any given time. It begs these questions: Why can we experience the best in some people and the worst in others? Why do things happen? What can we do about them, if anything? Humanity is a bit like a collection of cars. Each of these vehicles needs to be maintained and cared for, fine-tuned and fully functioning. We're responsible for our own vehicles that include our physiology, minds, and souls. From our souls comes a sense of self. To become conscious of it requires a discovery process.

From the moment we're born, we're set up for an experience in life. This includes a combination of the influences of family, peers, educators, and even strangers. Given this setup, we begin to self-identify as an expression of the sum of the parts.

Throughout our lives, we often believe what we are told. Most of what we're told causes a separation. The beliefs tend to place us in a box and compartmentalize us. We might say "I am a Dallas Cowboys' fan, a Green Bay Packers' fan, New Yorker, spelling-bee winner, or cheerleader." These identifiers become sounding boards as we thump our chests with pride, saying what it is we were programmed to say and feeling what it is we were programmed to feel. This identity lasts until that day when we begin to question the very nature of what was fed to us.

There may come a time in our lives when we say, "wait a minute, this doesn't feel right." We might begin to feel shy, scared, anxious, or other negative emotions that don't feel good and demand attention. When things begin stirring, we can step into the discovery phase of our lives. That's when we get in touch with our true essence. It might begin as a sense and then it evolves. Finally, there is a knowing that takes place in the aspect of who we are. This discovery is a pivotal aspect of personal growth.

The Role of Emotions

Emotions play the most crucial role through the discovery phase because they inform us if our current state of mind is positive or negative. They can signal to us a direction we might need to take to achieve personal happiness, peace of mind, or success. Getting in touch with our feelings is the key to creating change. When we are coping or running away from them, we will delay prospects for growth. We may even sabotage our development by staying stuck in a coping experience such as alcohol, drugs, or other addictive tendencies. When we break through, however, we are in a position to create lasting change.

Words we tell ourselves can lie but not our emotions. Deciphering feelings allows us to move in a direction that delivers peace of mind. The more comfortably we begin to navigate life, the more we can share our findings. These experiences become lessons from which others can also benefit. The discovery process and the emotional signals encountered, are lessons capable of being shared. Showing others a pathway to understanding the human experience is an act of love.

The final part of the way we work is sharing with others and contributing to a community. That community can be as small as our immediate family or as large as the global family. Perhaps one of the biggest changes we experience is a greater love for ourselves. That love needs an outlet because it must be expressed and shared to continue growing. Empowering others to be the best versions of themselves is an ideal outlet. When it's all said and done, the path from being programmed at birth to becoming authentic, is the path of truth. Emotions lead the way, and that's what this book is about.

An Anatomy of Choice

Emotional mastery is choosing reactions to circumstances and events. From the time an event occurs, to the actions taken regarding it, several steps take place. These steps provide an opportunity to exercise decisions that yield either peace or misery. Events happen to us all the time. They may be relationship related, environmentally stimulated, simple inconveniences or career and work issues. Things are always happening, and they stimulate responses; some of which will be more dramatic than others.

For each outside circumstance or event, we have a unique perceptual experience. For instance, we may be driving across town to see a friend and there could have been an accident on the highway, in which case traffic is at a standstill. If our perceptions are tuned to notice the worst in this situation, they may trigger anxiety. If our perceptions are tuned to see the experience as an opportunity to listen to calming music or make phone calls to friends, our emotional response might be neutral or even positive.

Our perceptions and beliefs about outside circumstances or events directly affect our emotions. They can make us sad, anxious, or angry. On the other hand, our perceptions and beliefs could trigger positive reactions such as happiness, freedom, or joy. It is important to listen to what our emotions are saying because they're sending a message that usually requires an action. There is nothing wrong with experiencing them as they arise. They simply happen. The question worth consideration becomes, "what can we do when the negative feelings arise?" We must resolve them to experience a life of peace and joy. Negative emotions require specific actions to move toward happiness.

We must carefully choose actions that direct us on a path to inner peace. We have options available, and the filters listed on the next page provide an understanding of the consequences of those actions. This chart illustrates the life-cycle of an emotional experience. We have flexibility every step of the way to affect the outcome. Being aware of this is the first step toward mastering our emotions. We must be committed to that awareness because we've realized we have no other choice if we want to be happy. Having already operated from left side of the Emotions Matrix has only led us to pain.

HOW TO MASTER EMOTIONS

SOMETHING HAPPENS
OUTSIDE EVENTS
OR CIRCUMSTANCES

GOES THRU WORLD VIEW FILTER
OUR EXISTING BELIEFS
OUR PERCEPTIONS
OUR SELF ESTEEM

GENERATES AN
EMOTIONAL RESPONSE
(AUTOMATIC)
Not right, not wrong

UNPLEASANT
DISTRAUGHT
ANGRY
DESPERATE

NEEDS ACTION
TO RESOLVE

PEACEFUL
OK
POSITIVE
RELAXED

NATURALLY MOVES
TOWARD

FEAR-BASED ACTIONS

Lead us toward
protection and defending

CONTROL
ATTACHMENTS
NEGATIVE BELIEFS
NEGATIVE MEANING MAKING
DEMANDS AND EXPECTATIONS
JUDGEMENTS

LOVE-BASED ACTIONS

Lead us toward
expression and creation

LETTING GO
ACCEPTANCE
POSITIVE PERCEPTIONS
GRATITUDE
EMPOWERING BELIEFS
POSITIVE SELF ESTEEM

DELIVERS

PAIN

INNER TURMOIL

BAD RELATIONSHIPS

MISERY

SICKNESS

DELIVERS

HARMONY

GOOD HEALTH

HEALTHY RELATIONSHIPS

JOY

INNER PEACE

Emotional Mastery

Emotions can be stimulated by outside events or circumstances. These are beyond our control, and are processed through our world view filter, which then generates an emotional response. This filter is comprised of, but not limited to, our existing beliefs, perceptions of the event itself, and self-esteem. These thoughts, perceptions and predispositions occur without much thought, and could be said to be part of our program.

Having gone through our knee-jerk processing, we then arrive at either an unpleasant or peaceful feeling, which has happened in a very automatic manner. They are not "right or wrong" reactions. We are simply responding to our world view filter, which must be addressed. Unpleasant reactions might result in fear, disgust, sadness, anger or frustration. Naturally, peaceful reactions deliver joy, happiness and satisfaction.

When we have negative emotional responses, it's our responsibility to resolve them in some way. They require action or processing for resolution. Our choices include moving toward positive actions that create peace in our lives, or toward negative ones, which continue delivering unhappiness.

Love-based actions, such as letting go, acceptance, positive perceptions, being in gratitude, empowering beliefs, and positive self-talk, create the space for joy. These actions deliver harmony, good health, good interpersonal relationships and peace. Fear-based actions such as control, attachments, negative beliefs, meaning-making, demands, expectations and judgments set the stage for misery. They deliver pain, inner turmoil, difficult relationships and poor health.

With improved perspective, we can make informed choices that deliver more happiness and peace than disappointment and upset. An indication of self-mastery is exhibited by the positive actions we take to deliver positive results. With continued application, we become more apt to choose by default that which delivers peace. Every time we feel something, there is an opportunity for increased self-awareness.

Choosing positive actions demands work, but it is well-rewarded by the results we achieve. Continuing to choose fear-based actions guarantees us continued frustrations and would beg the question, "who would choose that for themselves?"

CHAPTER 2

I THINK, THEREFORE I AM

"Dare to love yourself as if you were a rainbow with gold at both ends." - Aberjhani

Influences

In our mothers' wombs we begin to sense if we are loved. We come out of the womb with emotional predispositions and then immediately start taking cues from our surroundings and society. From youth, we begin to receive indications of our value, delivered by outsiders. These impressions are rarely under our control. We are more recipients of the information than freely chosen participants. The imprints interact with our personalities and we begin to develop or produce a sense of self-worth.

How we view the world interacts with our self-esteem and each affects the other. Lacking self-worth, we tend to focus on things that don't matter. We might spend more time causing unnecessary drama and gossiping, with less concern about making a difference in the world and taking responsibility for our own lives. This is an important discussion, because how we experience our value is a precursor to the lives we create.

Our World View

How we see ourselves affects our world view. When we see ourselves as valuable, we find value in the world. If we see ourselves as unworthy, we experience the opposite. From our perceptions, we develop beliefs that either empower or minimize us. Self-esteem can be viewed in many ways but fundamentally it comes down to our core sense of self. This sense will directly impact our emotional responses.

How we feel about ourselves stems from two sources. One is exterior; the experiences and interactions we have with society, communities, and the people who surround us. The other is an internal barometer with its own value metrics. When we feel like we're OK and we're worth something, we have positive self-esteem. When we don't feel valuable or worthy, we suffer from low self-esteem. This value conversation affects all our external relationships.

When we don't feel good about who we are, it's difficult to recognize the value of another. Oftentimes, we are unable to experience our true worth and find it easier to connect with it when someone else reflects it back. Others often reveal what we can't see in ourselves. Receiving this beneficial information can motivate us to do the same for others.

High self-esteem sets up pathways for the greatest amount of personal happiness in our lives. When we are happy, we spread more of it to others. Have you ever known a miserable person who's spreading light? Those who live joyfully, live fuller lives. People who live in emotional chaos experience life from an unfulfilling vantage point. Have you ever wanted to be around unhappy people? Typically, people seek their own kind. Thus, the adage, "misery enjoys company" has a ring of truth to it. It's hard to be that way alone and is best shared with others.

In our youth, positive self-esteem is made or destroyed by our families of origin and peers. For example, let's assume we grew up in a home where we were constantly abused and told we weren't pretty, smart, or worth anything. The origins of our self-worth would be very damaging, and we would most likely spend a percentage of our lives recovering. What we were taught about ourselves in our youth can cripple us in adulthood.

As we age, we become aware that the responsibility for creating a positive self-esteem is in our own hands. When we're unaware, we simply respond to the environment, taking in whatever is given. This is why so many get caught up in the cycle of self-identification shaped by comments and cues given by others. The choice of how we view ourselves is ours and it is incumbent upon us to take steps toward creating a positive self-image. Self-esteem is important because it becomes a filter for how we perceive everything around us. Thus, our personal happiness or misery is directly connected to how we see ourselves.

Life in Crisis – Bad boundary boss

Event:
Tony had been working as an assistant manager under his boss, Daryl, for 1 year at a large retail store. Over that year, he has taken more liberty to invade Tony's personal life and comment on it. Discovering that Tony is gay, Daryl flirted with him and began a process of poking fun and reading his personal texts. Tony allowed this to happen without reporting Daryl to human resources. However, every night he would go home to his roommates and complain about the situation at work. His friends and roommates spent countless hours advising Tony on appropriate actions to take. Despite the concern and excellent feedback, Tony did nothing. In fact, he

even flirted back, although Daryl was married with children. Eventually Daryl moved to another store and oddly enough, Tony both missed him and was glad he was gone. Tony never discussed this with HR.

Synopsis:
Tony's self-esteem was so low, he felt he deserved the treatment he received from Daryl. Tony didn't have a positive self-image. He felt more comfortable being abused than being treated well. He enjoyed being a victim. It gave him something to talk about with his friends. For someone with low self-esteem, the victimhood became his prize. His trophy in life is being mistreated. He's looking for sympathy and support from his roommates, but not so that he can change. Tony is just looking to be right and do nothing about it. At his core, he feels unworthy.

Reflections:
Tony is responsible for his self-respect, and if he doesn't concern himself with it, he can't expect anyone else to concern themselves either. We are singularly responsible for what we allow in our lives. Allowing mistreatment sends a signal that we are OK with what's happening, and it becomes our responsibility to stop it.

The way we allow others to treat us is an indication of how we perceive our worth. High self-worth tends to give birth to positive treatment just as low self-worth tends to birth negative. Whatever our beliefs, we look for situations to affirm their truths. People will sometimes test our self-esteem by pushing our buttons and observing how we value ourselves. We are deeply affected by what we consume. We can consume feelings of victimhood, being wronged, hostility and anger. We can also consume thoughts of possibilities, ideas, change, transformation, and celebration. The choice is ours.

One Thing Affects Another

Self-esteem is a crucial foundational determinant of whether we function from the left side or the right side of the emotion's matrix found on page 5. When we feel negatively about ourselves, we can't envision the positive and choose the left side of the chart, which delivers misery. Reacting positively would naturally have the opposite effect and always move us toward peace. To react positively, we would need to have a solid sense of our value, and that of others. There's no possible way we can have high self-esteem and at the same time look down on another. That is arrogance, not to be confused with self-esteem.

Life in Crisis – When management calls

Event:
Jose has been a manager in Boise, for a large company, for over 5 years. One day, his management team requested a meeting with him. He had a track record of being on time, his team loved him, and he approached this meeting with confidence, thinking he might be getting a raise. Other employees who had his work ethic had been ceremoniously rewarded with promotions and salary increases. When Jose walked into the meeting wearing his freshly pressed white shirt, he expected to be on the receiving end of great news. With the trademark smile on his face and his affable personality, he graciously greeted the team that had requested the meeting. Shocking to him, his direct manager chose to throw him under the bus with accusations and insinuations that he had not been performing his job well. With a puzzled look, Jose knew this was a moment where he would have to choose his words carefully. His perception was that he was doing a great job and that he missed out on some minor details that affected .1% of his job description instead of the 99.9% that he performed with

positive results. With a puzzled look on his face, Jose thought carefully before he replied. How he would choose to respond would either be from an empowered or a disempowered position. He chose to be empowered. He acknowledged the truth of the .1% and said he'd work on it and improve. He calmly discussed the situation, stood up, thanked the team for their time and left the room. Today was not the day that Jose would be taken down.

Synopsis:

Although Jose knew that he had been wronged, he also recognized that it was his responsibility to turn this negative situation into a positive in order to retain an excellent working relationship with the management team. Jose never allowed this event to negatively affect his self-esteem because he knew he had a quality of excellence in his work. The sense he made about the conversation helped him to frame the experience in a way that made him feel better about himself. He refused to take it personally and be disempowered. Had he chosen to react with anger, hostility, vengeance, retribution, or aggression, Jose would have lost the support of the team. Having exhibited calm behavior, today, Jose continues to be a vital manager in corporate America, having received a raise since that fateful day. He is respected by everyone and his former direct manager who threw him under the bus has already left for another position in the company. Jose's positive self-image guided him though very treacherous waters without a scratch.

What we tell ourselves about each conversation or event that occurs in our lives is either going to make us feel better or worse. So, why not frame experiences in a manner that accentuates the positive?

Choosing a Positive Reality

Our perspectives, beliefs, and self-image combine to affect our emotional realities. If they don't bring us peace, it's our responsibility to address them. Those with higher self-esteem value life to a degree that empowers them toward a more pleasant reality. Those with low self-esteem tend to act more from a victim mentality, believing that life happens to them and have limited motivation to change. It is important to remember that there are many ways of interpreting the same event and none of them are inherently right or wrong. There are simply the outcomes we get from the perspectives we choose. If we get to pick and choose our perceptions, why wouldn't we pick a way of looking at something that makes us feel better about ourselves?

False vs True Self-esteem

A false sense of self-esteem is realized when we believe we've "earned" it. This happens when our self-worth is determined by performance or somebody else's impressions. When we believe that doing something well makes us worthier, it's easy to become masters of creating false self-esteem. We often design "success formulas" based on the difficulties in life that had to be overcome. That formula may involve covering up our personal struggles with career success, looking good, fame, or financial wealth. It is a contrived source of self-esteem. Thinking that we'll feel better about ourselves because we're the wealthiest, smartest, fastest or most attractive is flawed. It's false because it's a measurement that lives outside of us.

True self-esteem lives within us. When we have it, acting out a role is no longer necessary. We don't have to prove anything or create a circus act to be noticed. True self-esteem is seeing the value in others as well as in ourselves. When we feel good about ourselves, we will have no need to degrade another or make someone less than. In fact, feeling good about ourselves propels us to feel good about others, because relationships are always a mirror to what's going on inside. Thinking highly of ourselves while not seeing the value in another, places us squarely on the road to narcissistic tendencies. Selfishness is only being concerned that our value is recognized.

Low vs. High Self-Image

Those with a low self-image may choose to inspire drama to avoid dealing with their own issues. They would tend to make everything a performance, which doesn't reflect their authentic selves. Not wanting the world to see the person they really are, they put on masquerade shows.

When we don't have internal strength and a strong sense of self, we often become theatrical because it's easier than facing the truth of who we really are. Low self-esteem can lead to a mindset that the world is happening "to us," "at us," or "against us." This thinking would generate a victim mentality and knee-jerk reactions.

Feeling worthless leads to an unstable foundation for life. It tends to produce an environment of over-personalization and thin-skinned responses. We can make mountains out of molehills when we desire attention but don't believe we deserve it. Since self-esteem is the primary contributor to our world views, having low self-esteem makes us feel negatively about ourselves and allows for mistreatment.

The alternative course of action for those of us with negative self-esteem is the disappearing act. We might feel like we don't deserve attention and become quiet, put on a hoodie, and sit in front of a video game for hours on end in a cold room. We don't have the motivation to go out and do things because we don't believe we will have positive results.

People with a high self-image tend to see the positive in the world. Accordingly, there is no motivation to mistreat people. All we must do is speak our truths quietly and firmly without theatrics or drama. Mistreating others can be driven from a position of low self-esteem because those with high self-esteem don't need to belittle someone to feel better about themselves.

Feeling good about ourselves allows us to be more present because we aren't concerned with being judged or evaluated. Everything is just an experience, and one which we don't take personally. We don't see ourselves as victims or persecutors. People with high self-esteem have no need for games, because we're not involved in "one-upping" anybody.

Improving Self-esteem

Why might we hold onto self-limiting beliefs that don't allow us to feel great? It's important to open our minds to different possibilities that reflect our value and begin to see ourselves in a positive light. Eliminating the lies and negative programming that we believe and replacing them with empowering thoughts is beneficial to our long-term happiness. Once we recognize that our self-esteem is lower than we'd like, there are options available to improve it. Oftentimes, the influence of others accelerates this process. When we dig deep and establish our worth, it grows like a deep-rooted tree. When others reflect our value, the experience can be more powerful than when we read about it in books and work on ourselves in isolation.

It's important to acknowledge those things that say, "I matter." When we feel uplifted, our views of life can change. What are some examples that communicate we matter? The considerations afforded to us by friends, colleagues, and family members are critical. Does someone listen to what we're saying? If they don't, we might need to consider if they're actually diminishing our self-esteem. Determining who belongs in our inner circle can go a long way toward improving our self-image.

Outside Circumstances vs our Sense of Self

There is an external component to self-esteem (how others treat us) that interacts with our internal sense of self. We weigh external circumstances and events against our internal barometer of how we feel about ourselves to deliver an emotional outcome. Honor is the experience of our external circumstances matching or exceeding our internal barometer. Dishonor is when the external does not match our internal and someone doesn't value us the way we see ourselves. When we're honored, we experience greater power. When we're dishonored, we experience disempowerment.

Conclusion

Self-esteem is at the core of our lives, affecting all its aspects. Our ability to love others is influenced by how we love ourselves. It impacts all our interpersonal interactions. Working on our issues and improving how we feel about ourselves places us in a better position to contribute to the improved self-image of others. Making a difference in other people's lives is an important indicator that we matter and at the same time, enhances our own well-being.

Expressions of Self-esteem

• Our beliefs contribute to our self-esteem as much as the other way around. Whatever we believe has the power to affect how we feel about ourselves.

• Self-esteem reflects the value we see in ourselves. It could easily be interchanged with the term "self-value." Self-esteem affects relationships because we attract according to how we see ourselves.

• When we have low self-esteem, we can see the beauty in life, but we can't feast on it. It's more of an observation than it is an indulgence.

• High self-esteem stems from a solid inner foundation that gives us a spring-board to experience joy, power, and creation.

• Others may influence our self-esteem, but we are ultimately responsible for it.

Language of Self-esteem

"My inner reality creates my outer reality."

CHAPTER 3

SUCCESS REIMAGINED

*"Emotions have immense power. This power can propel you
towards your dreams and goals, or sabotage and ruin your life.
Choose wisely how to use the power of your emotions."*
- Stan Jacobs

What is Success?

Success and failure are both illusions, designed to either deliver
or rob us of dignity and self-esteem. Unfortunately, they are
external measurements designed to help us feel better or worse
about ourselves. Success provides an opportunity to hero-
worship or appoint ourselves heroes. Identifying with failure
sets us up to be wrong, less than, or confirms an already low
sense of self. These terms are arbitrary and serve little to no
purpose to those who are emotionally self-reliant. A lot of
people think "when I'm successful, I'll be at peace."
Traditional views of success don't deliver peace of mind, as
evidenced by countless successful celebrities and individuals,
still striving for inner peace.

Success is typically considered the attainment of that which we desire. Whatever it may be: the championship, the CEO position, the house on the corner, and even inner peace. When we achieve the elusive dream, we are considered "successful." There are two distinct ways of defining or viewing success and whichever we choose creates either fleeting moments of happiness or an enduring inner peace.

Traditional Views of Success

Success is one of those words that we seldom challenge, because it's been ingrained in us since birth. Traditional views might include financial qualifications, such as how much a person is worth, or how much they make. We place a lot of emphasis on salaries, size of homes and the ability to write large checks to charitable causes. We "ooh and ahh" at the lifestyles of the rich and famous. We admire those who have awards and honors; academic achievement, certifications and credibility. We see fame, celebrity, glamour and notoriety as statements of success, and applaud those people with a silent wish that we had their lives. For some, success is having a family, an amazing physique, beauty or materialistic things.

Social media has upped the ante regarding success. We now count the number of likes, followers, shares, or our number of contacts. Those with higher numbers are perceived as more desirable. We strive to be noticed by highly influential people. Will they like our comments and respond to them on their page of hundreds of thousands of followers? When they do, we consider that success as well. The scale of reach is an indication of success because it means we are important, and others want to tune in to our lives and conversations. These are considered accomplishments, and we tally them daily to assess our standing within society.

We share stories of our net worth, trust funds, real estate holdings and legacies. With pride, we recall our endowments to universities. Yes, we spend a great deal of energy consumed with appearing successful in the eyes of the world. I wonder how many of us even consider how powerfully the illusion and allure of success controls our lives. For some, success even looks like the partner we choose. The pedigreed significant other can make us feel like we've arrived as a power-couple. The publicity we garner, or notoriety we inspire are also measuring sticks. While there is nothing wrong with all these delightful things happening, they are all external sources of success that make us feel good. They deliver fleeting happiness, because the landscape is always changing.

Traditional views of success mean that we can congratulate ourselves when we're superior to the competition. Its roots stem from a comparative nature, which means my head can only be higher, when your head is lower. This type of thinking leads to competitive qualities, striving, constant comparisons and the inability to feel good about ourselves unless we outrank another. It results in big egos as well as depression.

On the opposite side of success, we must consider failure. The paradigm suggests that if I am not successful, then by definition, I must be a failure, or at best, less successful than someone else. In either case, we're in a race against others to determine where we stand. Yet, with achievements and accomplishments so important to our egos, is there a way out of this crippling paradigm? There's nothing wrong with being successful. The problem is when we identify with it as the source of our self-esteem. What might be an alternate way of viewing success, such that it is not dependent upon outside metrics?

Success Redefined

There is another way to define success, that has nothing to do with the traditional standards to which we've grown accustomed. This is more of an inner journey; one that forces us to look inside and see how we live. It's about a race against self, rather than a race against someone else. In this view of success, we become masters of our emotions, able to handle ourselves in every situation. We are emotionally self-reliant, not seeking someone or something to fulfill us, because we know we're enough. We don't need awards and accolades because we're not concerned with outside appearances. Being home to ourselves means there's no need to seek distinctions within society. If they come, fine; but they don't affect our self-esteem either way.

This way of thinking means we desire everyone to be equally successful, because it's about us versus ourselves and whether we have the will to be fully expressed. Our only concern is how we can improve on yesterday to become a better version of ourselves. We seek fairness, understanding of others, generosity and gratitude. Success now means the degree to which we honor internal desires, needs and how well our outsides match our insides. We assess our capacity to honor others and earnestly seek that quality. Going deeper, we recognize the desire to share good feelings, wisdom and gifts with the world as an expression of a successful life.

Now, we celebrate completing projects, contributing to local and global initiatives and being the person who leaves things better than how we found them. We survey our insides and discover that we have integrity; we do what we say and say what we do. There is no need to lie in this paradigm of success, because we know where we stand within ourselves. We are liberated from competitive striving, envy and ego-building. We express compassion for others, knowing we're all in this together. We satisfy our hearts desires, motivated to fulfill our purpose.

Emotions Provide the Answers

Analyzing and understanding our feelings leads to emotional mastery, which becomes a foundation for success. If we want to master our emotions, we must begin to know ourselves better. Unpleasant emotions tell an important story. They serve as an indicator that an ineffective perception is operating within us. Positive ones move us toward peace and happiness. In the English language there are over 3000 words describing emotions. Two-thirds of them are negative, while only one-third are positive. Therefore, it's clear from the get-go that society exhibits more tendencies toward the negative. Since life is impacted greatly by our emotions, we must make a concerted effort to master them. Unfortunately, we often lack the tools necessary to shape these experiences. We want to reduce our reactive nature and increase our interactive nature with emotions to establish greater peace of mind.

When emotions control us, we are enslaved and react irrationally. They contain hidden messages that are a call to action. These messages may seem unpleasant when not understood. Deciphering them can minimize our upset. When we don't have words for what we're experiencing, we can study our emotions for insights. They act as an early warning system, signaling what we value and our personal truths. Emotions must be addressed, one way or another.

Inner Chaos, Outer Calm

So, is there anything we can do in the middle of chaos? The first thing to consider is a perceptual change that would convert it to a positive or neutral experience. We may have a knee-jerk reaction because our perceptions are fixated on a narrow or familiar view of the situation. We must change our relationship to the event to change our experience. One way of accomplishing this is by altering our perceptions or identifying possible negative outcomes if we remain in the current emotional state.

Negative emotions that might affect us include: frustration, anger, hurt, depression, grief, fear, loneliness, and isolation. They often manifest as envy, guilt, regret, and remorse. These are all repercussions of a distorted world view. The problems that ensue can show up as disconnected relationships, victim identification, unhappiness, and dissatisfaction with life. Unaddressed emotions live inside and have adverse effects.

We can also express positive emotions that require no resolution, such as joy, satisfaction, and happiness. All these ultimately lead to peace and serenity. They create the possibility for deep and meaningful relationships. Living joyfully, we can readily identify and step into spontaneous opportunities because we are fully present to what's happening.

Emotional Mastery is a Pathway to Success

The foundation for creating a dream life starts with achieving emotional mastery. When we connect with our emotions and respond with love, we can positively affect the future. Without that connection, it's difficult to move from a life in chaos, to a life of inner peace. Being in control of our emotions sets the stage for making informed choices. This sets us up for a successful life; one lived from the vantage point of a strong, peaceful foundation. We often discover that traditional views of success and failure distance us from a life of inner peace and leave us longing for more.

Playing by the traditional views of success creates an external dependency for happiness. We must change our views of success to experience serenity. A continual experience of not being successful in the traditional sense would eventually damage our self-esteem and prevent connection with our power.

Whenever our happiness is delivered by something that lives on the outside, it resides in someone else's hands. Surveying our possessions, partners and lives without qualifying any of it as success or failure, sets us up for an alternate view of success. In order to get there, however, we must go through the fears and actions that control us today. To conquer success, we must learn to define it differently - on our own terms.

PART II

7 Obstacles to Peace

"Happy people find a way to live with their problems, and miserable people let their problems stop them from living."
- Sonya Parker

CHAPTER 4

THE DESTRUCTIVE POWER OF FEAR

"Everything you want is on the other side of fear."
- Jack Canfield

Fear Defined

The dictionary defines fear as "an unpleasant emotion caused by the belief that someone or something is dangerous, likely to cause pain, or a threat." It can be considered a messenger that informs us that something isn't right, or an instinct that is a call to action. Living in fear is disempowering and can also be a motivation to change. It signals that it's time to confront an issue. Oftentimes, we aren't afraid of the fear itself, but instead we are doubtful of our ability to overcome it.

Fear can be imprinted or absorbed, almost as if it's in our DNA. We observe how our parents respond to life and we begin to respond the same way. As such, fear can be said to be programmed or passed down generationally. It lives in the body as well as the mind. It can be stored in cellular memory from trauma. Fear keeps us small and minimizes our potential because we feel like we're not powerful enough.

A Life of Fear

There are essentially two ways of approaching life. One way is from a position of fear and the other is from love. Fear keeps us frozen and stagnant, inhibiting our movement toward self-discovery. This can result in child-like tendencies such as entitlement, always being right, and irresponsibility. In fact, this typically causes relinquishment of personal responsibility for happiness as we place it on someone else. Further effects include being disconnected, lacking self-control, and believing that we're not OK. A fundamental experience of fear is that the outside poses a bigger threat than the inside can handle. This can keep us relegated to our comfort zones and separate from a world of new possibilities.

Being afraid keeps us locked in old patterns, unaware and oblivious. These patterns may express themselves as choices that result in controlling behaviors, intense attachments, judgment of others, negative self-beliefs, negative meaning-making and uncompromising demands. Ultimately of course, these actions are a super-highway to pain, difficult relationships, and eventually misery. It's important to become familiar with fear and how it operates, to move beyond it.

What Fear Tells Us

Sometimes when we want something very badly, we make ourselves anxious. Our excitement can become so intense that it turns into fear. Let's assume we feel a strong attraction towards someone but resist initiating a conversation. There is tremendous excitement to strike up a dialogue but then fear about what they might think enters the picture. Uncertainty about their potential reaction might keep us in a frozen state of non-action.

This is an indication that we are in a state of self-doubt, or that we have placed someone's head higher than our own. It is telling us that we don't fully believe in our ability to handle a situation. We amplify the significance and make it seem like it's a huge event that may seriously impact the course of our lives. By overestimating a single moment, we trick ourselves into believing in fears power to shape our future. In this manner, fear acts as an informant about where we stand in our level of personal development. Our perspective is limited by the inability to see beyond our inadequacies.

The message fear communicates is that we must learn to recognize our value and develop beliefs that are empowering. It tells us that when we don't have faith in ourselves, we cannot achieve our desires. Without trusting ourselves we will miss out on potentially life-changing opportunities. We are not designed to run away and hide from that which inspires us. These intense feelings that show up from nowhere are signals guiding us toward a more fulfilling life. The challenge lies in appropriately responding to the emotions we're experiencing in the moment. Living with fear magnifies our perceived incompetency's and leaves us feeling powerless to improve our lives.

Why We Fear

Fear has multiple root causes and can be learned or passed from parent to child. It can be an emotional response to a belief that has been instilled upon us from religion, friends, family, etc. We might develop a fear because we are impressionable and allow others to influence our thoughts and emotions. There may also be an empathic quality to fear, because it is energetic and can be sensed and felt. Some of us are so sensitive that we may be picking up on emotions going on around us, both positive and negative.

When we believe in our personal power, we will not be afraid. Those of us who are brought up not believing in that power are being conditioned to activate fear. Observing circumstances or media coverage can stimulate this feeling. If we're constantly instructed to be vigilant because of possible terrorist acts, we might be scared going to public places.

A lot of things we label as "fear" might also have their origins in doubt. Any doubt that was not overcome can lead us in that direction. For instance, if we think that we can't hit in a baseball game with spectator's present, we might begin to feel anxious going to the plate to bat. We may identify with the idea that we are not enough. What might it mean to our team, our community, or our peer group if we fail?

Fear attempts to humiliate us and makes us look pathetic. We might choose to remain stuck because it is out of our comfort zone to face fear directly. Being scared can act as an excuse to not confront our issues. What we might be saying is, "I just can't do it," but what we really mean is, "I'm not in enough pain to want to change." We can create excuses to justify our stagnation. A feeling of inadequacy is at the root of it. If we don't believe in ourselves, fear always wins.

The Negative Effects of Fear

Chronic and ongoing anxiety may activate evasive tactics and cause us to be in constant "management" mode of our emotions. This can take a great deal of energy and cripple our development. Continuously dwelling on fear adds fuel to the fire and deprives us of opportunities that could bring joy and happiness. From the vantage point of living a small life, we become diminished, cowering, frightened and immobilized. This kind of life is really a reflection of living in the most artificial of ways.

Living with fear robs us of the opportunity to improve our self-esteem and is a static reminder of our inability to change our lives for the better. It keeps us in hiding and prevents us from living a connected life. When we live this way, we lose the part of ourselves that is worth saving the most – our power to create. When we hide that part, we cheat ourselves out of an authentic experience of being proud. We might start to feel trapped in a way of being that doesn't accurately represent our true self. As fear keeps us from actively jumping into life, we might become spectators, sitting on the sidelines, waiting for something to happen, instead of taking personal initiative. In life, we're either watching or creating!

Insecurity is one of fear's many faces and breeds envy and doubt into its victims. It can cause us to undermine others who are more successful. When we fear something, we instantly give it power. This prevents us from determining our own fate, and places us at the mercy of something or someone that might not have our best interests in mind. When we see fear as a beast that is bigger and braver than we are, we diminish ourselves and are choosing to be ruled by a dictator who keeps us small and underdeveloped. We appear scared and insecure when we don't believe in ourselves. How can anyone else trust us if we don't trust in ourselves? What is not faced, expands and reflects our inability to make peace with something. It communicates that we lack a fundamental belief in self to handle events and situations.

Resolving Fear

To overcome fear, we must face it. When we are brave enough to confront our demons, they instantly start to lose their power. In that moment we begin to realize that we are capable of overcoming challenges which at first seemed daunting. Only in facing and addressing our fears do we discover our true potential. It takes great courage to confront something that appears bigger than life. The best way to eradicate fear is to create an inner environment that is solid and unshakable. We must be grounded in beliefs that are positive and empowering. Our self-esteem must be strong, and we must see the world from higher vantage points if we are to prosper.

Standing on solid ground, we can see that many of the reasons we thought we should be afraid were unfounded. It takes courage to walk through the dark places of the soul, and we must be willing leave our comfort zones. When we take action, we are pulled from the imaginings of our minds and put into a reality where we can see that our fears were irrational all along.

Fear indicates that an underlying belief is operational. Our job is to identify that belief and handle it before it handles us. All emotions serve as indicators and the path to peace mandates that we address them. To summon the courage within is to acknowledge that we are stronger than we could ever imagine. This type of courage is necessary for the annihilation of our fears and trembling. We must ignite the spark of love that connects us to a sublime sense of self that can overcome and accomplish anything. The way out of fear is love.

KEY PAIN POINTS OF FEAR

- The more we fear something, the more power we give it, and the bigger it becomes. It will continue to keep us small for as long as we allow.
- If we are afraid to live our lives, what kind of life are we living?
- The more we confront what we're afraid of, the less of an effect it will have on us.
- We are impressed by fearlessness and courage and yet we are so afraid to become these things.
- Fear is about doubting our ability to deal with a perceived external threat.
- Courageous acts can only be performed when fear is present.

Language of Fear

"I'm afraid because I believe I'm smaller than the challenge facing me."

CHAPTER 5

HANDCUFFED TO DESIRE

"Attachment is the great fabricator of illusions; reality can be obtained only by someone who is detached."
- Simone Weil

What is Attachment?

Attachment can be defined as a strong, emotional, and binding tie to someone or something. It has the quality of wanting to firmly hold onto a person, fantasy, or thing, combined with a strong resistance to letting go. Attachments do not serve us because they inevitably result in pain. The inability to accept things "as they are," delivers endless misery. The willingness to accept circumstances indicates our degree of emotional mastery. A spirit of scarcity creates a fertile environment for attachment to thrive.

Anxieties can be triggered by believing that we can't live without a desired object or outcome. This is the nature of attachment, which stems from an inability to be OK without getting what we want. That desperate feeling is the result of not trusting ourselves and our own power.

The Nature of Attachment

Attachments will always bind us to the object or circumstance of our desire. Whether it's a lifestyle, a way of being, or a person – whatever we're attached to creates a dependency. We are not particularly interested in other options and most often do not even have eyes for alternatives. We have made a specific person, place, or thing, our savior at that moment. That experience is the only thing that will bring us a sense of completeness and serves as an indication that we are not grounded. A self-reliant person would not need to lean on someone else for their happiness. Surrendering our personal power to someone else is debilitating. Our sense of happiness and feeling complete are at the mercy of any attachment.

The habit of manipulating others to satisfy our desires is commonplace for those living in emotional poverty. Dependence on others sets the stage for manipulative relationships. A desperate person will do whatever is necessary to get their needs met. When we lean on others, we are no longer functioning independently and are in bondage to them because a healthy middle-ground is absent.

A stubborn, "all or nothing" nature keeps us locked in a cycle that delivers either pain or pleasure, and nothing in-between. When we're attached, we will often exploit others to get what we want. It can feel like a race for survival, or even like a matter of life and death as we pursue a desired object.

Tasting something so good might cause us to believe that nowhere else could that fruit taste as sweet and juicy. We can amplify it by creating the context that makes it, "the ultimate experience." When our minds can perceive of nothing better, the conditions for attachment are ripe. The opposite of attachment is aversion. To have a strong aversion towards something or someone is similar to a strong attachment. Only in equanimity can we truly experience emotional freedom. Our stubbornness causes us to view things from one specific perspective. This diminishes our ability to see other potential outcomes, which could deliver happiness.

Life in Crisis - Help me, Rhonda!

Event:
Rhonda is a 36-year-old single woman living in the Gold Coast of Chicago. She attended Purdue University and was raised in a large family where she didn't receive much attention. Rhonda enjoys shopping at Neiman Marcus on Michigan Ave. and is always sporting the most current fashion. Over a hundred shoe styles embellish her wardrobe. She's sad more often than she'd like to be and is constantly in a state of comparison. She chooses her friends based on what they look like rather than their character. Thus, she finds herself alone most evenings longing for connection and attention.

Starting her day is like preparation for war, and beauty is the battlefield. The most expensive brands of cosmetics and perfumes adorn her bathroom. She spends 2 hours strategizing the optimal look to gain the attention of others. She carefully selects beauty supplies so that at any moment, she can refresh her look. While she's out and about, she notices all the other beautiful people and compares herself. She skims over the average looking people, barely noticing them, until she finally glances on someone compelling enough to capture her attention. She admires their beauty from afar, imagining how great that person's life must be. She stops for a moment and feels sadness in her heart. Feeling like there's something missing in her life, she ponders what it could be. Let's find out what it is...

Synopsis:

Rhonda is attached to the image she presents to the world. She desperately wants to be seen. By caring so much about how she looks, she causes herself an abundance of worry which delivers unnecessary anxiety and sadness. Her life is a constant comparison. She is either better than or worse than everyone with whom she comes in contact. By living this way, she experiences constant striving for the best products and looks available. Hers is a life of constant craving.

Comparisons are divisive. A low self-image is at the core of her attachment to how others might view her. Being attached to outer beauty keeps Rhonda grasping for her purse to feel better. This strategy tends to create more problems than it solves because it keeps Rhonda locked in an analytical and comparative cycle. If Rhonda let go of her attachments to "looking good," and accepted herself as being enough, there would be no anxiety. Over time, this stress adds more wrinkles to her face, causing her to become even more dependent on her make-up. Rhonda's attachments make it hard for her to find peace within herself. If she could ever let go, she would find a sense of freedom that she's never quite experienced before and she'd clutch her purse just a bit less fervently.

Attachments can be the result of our perceived inadequacies. Rhonda is just one example, but we need look no further than our own set of friends and closets filled with clothes, shoes and cosmetics, to witness the effects of this behavior. Until we are self-reliant, we will hunger for what we want. Low self-esteem and minimal self-reliance produce a predisposition for this to occur.

Why We Become Attached

We may have known what emotional bankruptcy, deprivation, and uncertainty feels like. We may have also felt the pain of rejection. When someone enters our lives and flips that pain to incredible pleasure, this causes an intense high that we don't ever want to end! We may even try and control them. When making prisoners out of those who deliver joy, we deny ourselves the ultimate pleasure of being freely chosen.

Having a clear and uncompromising hunger can blind us to the extent that it controls us. Ultimate certainty and strong convictions can create blinders to other possibilities. We can be clear about the things we want and develop a blind-spot to how we've become bonded to them. Ultimately, this limits and enslaves us.

The feeling that we get can be so intense that it keeps us going back for more because there's nothing like it. The payoff is high and the feel-good is intense. Our real attachment is to the feelings we get, rather than to the object itself. The feeling is so unlike anything we've felt. Consider the lonely woman who hasn't had a boyfriend in 10 years. She meets the guy of her dreams who treats her fantastically, and now she doesn't want to live without him. It makes sense why she longed for his company. The payoff is huge but so are the consequences. The highest highs will always deliver the lowest lows.

Life in Crisis - How do you solve a problem like Maria?

Event:
Maria lives in San Diego, is 28 years old and hasn't had a serious boyfriend since she was a senior at Southern Cal. She's dated a bit, but the dates have left her feeling empty and unfulfilled. She's a live wire. She likes to go out, works hard,

does Cross-fit, and lives alone in a condo she bought 2 years ago. Her home is beautiful. The inside is perfectly appointed, and every piece of furniture knows its place. The scents from the candles she burns are always seasonal and her decorations are impeccable, especially for the holidays. And yet, if you walked into her apartment, you would immediately feel the loneliness. Then along came Chris, a 32-year-old investment banker, whom she met while doing Cross-fit. He is a graduate of Harvard, with a fantastic resume, handsome, and sports a 6-pack. They hit it off and have been dating for 3 months.

During the first two weeks of their relationship, Maria became increasingly interested and showed it through the amount of text messages she sent Chris. He would respond to half of them and when he wouldn't respond, she would experience anxiety and panic-attacks. She would invite herself over and interrupt his plans so that they could be together. She needs constant assurances of his affections. She is always inventing reasons for them to be together, such as going to plays, sporting events, dinners, etc. Despite all the signals that Chris needs space from her, it is Maria's fantasy that they will wind up together. She never thought she would meet a guy like him. He is charming, handsome, romantic, and successful. He is any woman's dream come true. It wasn't long before she said those 3 little magic words. She fell head-over-heels and to her, he is "the one." Chris thought things were alright but wanted to keep his options open. He wanted to see where things would go and take the relationship day by day. When he felt Maria starting to get too clingy, he began to pull back and now wants to see her less. He will eventually break up with her, and this will devastate Maria. Where did Maria go wrong?

Synopsis:
As Maria became more attached to Chris, she became more miserable. While under the delusion of being in love, she

sacrificed her ability to generate true happiness for herself and became completely dependent on Chris for her emotional well-being. By qualifying her relationship with Chris as, "the best she's ever had," her attachment began to manifest. Considering it a superlative experience set her up for the attachment. She refused to read the signals he was sending and didn't even consider any other possibilities besides marriage. She couldn't imagine life without him. In a very real way, she created the pleasure/pain pendulum. Since he was the only one who could give her pleasure, not having Chris would also give Maria the ultimate pain. Maria's attachment made her needy and ultimately drove Chris away. Had Maria not been attached to him, she wouldn't have been so clingy. Instead of simply enjoying the good times they shared, Maria conceived a fantasy world in her head that she had to have Chris the way she wanted him. Obviously when that didn't happen, the only experience left was painful. Loving herself first would have set the foundation for a stable and balanced relationship.

By making another person responsible for our happiness, we thrust onto them the burden of taking care of our emotional well-being. Other people aren't here to oversee and maintain the state of our happiness. They are only responsible for themselves, as we are responsible for ourselves. Requiring someone to behave according to our desires is the true source of our suffering. When blaming another person for our emotional state, we miss a golden opportunity to learn more about the true source of our reactions, and a chance at real personal growth.

Staying attached is common when we believe it's better to have the familiar than to potentially have nothing. We may think that however unsatisfying a relationship may be, it still beats the alternative of having no one. In reality, being alone could be exactly what we need.

Consequences of Attachment

Attachments cloud our realities when we pursue someone to fulfill our fantasies rather than to love authentically. Naturally, this sets us up for tremendous failure. It's as if we're more concerned with our storybook ending, than being in relationship with a whole and independent person! We enter those "relationships," (better called fantasies) with a mythology in our heads of a specific archetype we want to show up in our life. Will my significant other be the hero, heroine, trickster, or guardian?

Who can possibly fill the shoes of our unrealistic fantasies? As such, lovers become more like characters in our novel than real people with whom we're authentically engaged. Our dream ending of the story means we try to make someone fit the character and act in accordance with our desires. When we realize they're human and have their own mind, they lose that magical quality that we attributed to them in the first place, and we grieve the loss of the imagination. Attachment to romantic ideals often leads to sadness.

Dire consequences await those who live this way. The lows are devastating and often leave indelible marks. In a way, we set up a hopeless scenario from the start because being attached means never having enough of what we seek. The dependent and leaning nature can lead us down a path in which we have given away our well-being for a dream. In doing so, we've made ourselves vulnerable and placed a target on our hearts.

It's easier to be hurt when we desire a specific result. In fact, being neutral about an experience would be much less volatile. Unable to exhibit a neutral position guarantees upset because the heart is always searching for the elusive magic.

Whatever we're attached to becomes our personal prison cell. In this way, we become enslaved and live a tormented life. A sense of entitlement, a selfish nature, or fears of deprivation are all cornerstones of attachment. Each of these causes a loss of control or an abdication of control to someone or something else. Anytime our happiness is contingent upon another person or a desired outcome, all bets are off on our true peace of mind.

Life in Crisis – Jack's in a box

Event:
Jack is a manager at a Chipotle restaurant in Houston. He rose through the ranks quickly and is a 22-year-old high school graduate, currently attending community college. Jack aspires to be a regional manager of Chipotle one day. He was an "A" student in high-school, comes from humble beginnings and has worked hard for everything in his life. He supports his family and manages everything in life by a routine. Everything works on schedule and on demand. When Jack joined Chipotle, he bought into the system and understood that it is everything. Being that guy, Jack sees everything in black and white and is very attached to protocol and how people perform their functions. He has a reputation for constantly correcting his staff on the smallest of details. The turnover at his restaurant is 3 times the national average and the regional manager is on his way to deliver a warning to Jack. What happened to Jack, the rising star?

Synopsis:
Since Jack is attached to the most efficient outcome, he is unbending and non-negotiable in how tasks are to be performed. He is considered a micro-manager by the team and they resent his constant bickering and nit-picking. Often, the restaurant is so busy that there isn't time to do each task exactly by the book. When Jack blows up, he alienates the staff. Though

he thinks he's doing everything "right," because it's by the book, his attachment is more to the process than to the team morale. Jack is so concerned with the way things "should be done," that he has a huge blind-spot regarding what's really important – the employees. When a manager is attached to process over performance, he or she is certain to alienate the staff through micro-management. The team senses the manager's concern with prioritizing processes over employee development.

People can feel when they're appreciated and when they're used. Personal creativity and professional initiatives are thwarted by Jack. The funny thing is, bosses like this may wonder why their employees aren't coming up with new ideas on their own. Who can come up with new ideas in an environment where you're constantly berated and held accountable to process standards? Nobody wants to be told how to do everything. Subordinates typically want guidance and support, without taking away their personal style. Another interesting fact is that although the employees can often see things that managers can't, they may resist sharing those insights when they know management already has "their" way of doing things. Jack misses out on all kinds of good information that could enhance his performance. Don't be like Jack!

Costs of Attachment

Attachments create anxiety and cause us to negatively perceive our environment. We begin noticing everything wrong in our lives, which further adds to our already depleted emotional state. We may get stuck in a vicious cycle of negativity.

Whatever we're attached to keeps us returning to the scene of the crime and affects all our relationships. We're guaranteed to keep experiencing pain as long as we remain anchored by attachments. This holding pattern doesn't allow for any spontaneous gifts that might be in store. It diminishes inner-peace and bonds us to either old desires or old hungers that drove us there in the first place.

KEY PAIN POINTS OF ATTACHMENT

- Attachment means living in a constant pendulum swing of emotions.
- Inflexibility silences the voices of others.
- Manipulation and games are used to satisfy the person attached. This leads to inauthentic relationships that people will avoid at all costs.
- Being attached can give birth to a narrow-minded headset, which inhibits the ability to see the bigger picture.
- We can be attached to ideas and plans of action. This can create tension and interpersonal conflict with others.

Language of Attachment

"I know what I want and where I am going. If I don't get it, I'm going to be upset."

"I want what I want, when I want it."

CHAPTER 6

CONTROL FREAKS

"Because to take away a man's freedom of choice, even his freedom to make the wrong choice, is to manipulate him as though he were a puppet and not a person."
- Madeleine L'Engle

The Nature of Control

Control is a way of arranging people or events to fit our liking and originates from a self-centered nature. When we are in this mode we are more concerned with managing situations and people and less concerned about how it affects them. Acting as a decoy, it keeps us from having to face what's really going on inside of us.

We might get angry when someone doesn't behave the way we demand. Our anger doesn't stem from their actions, but from our need for compliance. By not allowing people the freedom to act in ways that suit them, we upset ourselves by imagining what we think they "should do." It's arrogant to assume that we know what's best, and get worked up when someone doesn't perform according to our direction! A controlling nature is an indication of lacking peace within ourselves. When we don't take care of our emotions, we learn to control the environment to feel OK.

As we impose forceful behaviors onto others, we will usually be met with resistance. Directing others to behave certain ways, we are faced with frustration because most people want freedom. By discounting their ability to act freely, we are sending the message that we know better and our opinions matter more. Healthy-minded people do not want to sacrifice independence to be in a relationship with a controlling person. A prisoner's natural instinct is to escape!

Life in Crisis – Bed-time for Sally

Event:

Sally and Mark live together in a one-bedroom apartment in the Upper West Side of New York City. Mark wakes up every morning at 5:00 a.m. to work out and then heads straight to work. As a stockbroker, he takes on extra stress for extra pay. When Mark, who is 40, finally comes home after a long day at the office, he is ready to eat, watch T.V., and go to bed. Sally, on the other hand, is a spunky 30-year old with many hobbies and works part-time at the neighborhood pet shop. She enjoys watching late-night television and going out with her friends on the weekends. When 9:00 p.m. rolls around and Mark is just about ready for bed, he calls upon Sally to sleep next to him. Not being tired, she resists his demands. This causes Mark to make it a big deal and they end up bickering. This is usually enough to wear Mark down to the point to where he passes out and forgets the whole thing until the next day. Sally is also equally worn out from the argument and usually ends up falling asleep shortly thereafter. Let's take a look at what is really going on.

Synopsis:

Mark's real upset doesn't arise from Sally wanting to stay awake, but from not getting his way. Essentially, the upset is something Mark does to himself. He is fully responsible for the *pain he experiences. That doesn't mean he's not entitled to his desires. It just means that trying to force them on Sally will cause him to suffer unless he gets his way. In this scenario, there is little to no wiggle room for Sally to make her own choices. She is dictated how to behave and must conform. The outcome can only spell disaster. Sometimes we try to control objects, people, or situations to make ourselves happy. Mark wants Sally to be happy, but also wants her definition of happiness to match his. Mark can't even see that there's anything wrong with that. He will get it eventually, but by then, Sally may have found an alternative sleeping arrangement. How's that empty Tempur-pedic feel now, Mark?*

Sometimes, when we can't handle the thought of being out of control, we attempt to manage our environment to generate a sense of calm. This behavior is also exhibited in people who feel the need to control conversations. Have you ever spoken with someone who just won't let go of their air time to speak? They speak over you, around you, and seldom do they hear you. These conversations appear more like power struggles than genuine interactions.

Life in Crisis – A Whirlwind in the Windy City

Event:
Raphael was having a group of people meet in downtown Chicago after work to celebrate his promotion. It was a group of professional colleagues totaling 8 people, and Raphael set the agenda for the evening. Everything was fine until early dinner-time. The group was moving slowly, everyone at their own pace, enjoying cocktails at a bar with a great downtown view. Raphael had made plans for dinner at Morton's at 8:00 p.m. sharp. Nobody else was looking at the time and it was 7:45 p.m. when Raphael began to stress. He informed the group that they had to finish their drinks and that he was leaving in 5

minutes with or without them, and that 2 Uber's would be waiting for them downstairs. Two of the group members saw a client at the bar and had engaged in an important conversation. Raphael interrupted their discussion insisting that "it's time to go, NOW!" Disturbed and angered, the two chose to abandon the plans for Raphael's celebration. Now Raphael's evening celebration was ruined, and he had no one to blame but himself. The mood of the party became very tense, and those who knew Raphael began to roll their eyes, saying, "He's at it again."

Synopsis:

Raphael suffers from tremendous anxiety. When he is not in control, he senses that he is out of control. For Raphael, the world revolves around his agendas, leadership and guidance. When someone deviates, Raphael pulls back the reigns to establish his dominance. He has not learned how to manage his anxiety, so he tries managing the world around him. Ultimately, for Raphael to feel comfortable, he must manage one or the other. By taking on the role of deciding what everyone should be doing, he has caused unnecessary frustration for himself and tension for everyone else. Raphael can't even count on his 8 closest colleagues to stick with him through dinner. He must deal with his internal issues to rectify his controlling nature. Anything short of that, he'll keep alienating his relationships.

Reflections:

There is a point that can be made to support Raphael's frustration with the lack of support exhibited by his colleagues. Clearly, it's his promotion party, and there are times in life, when we make efforts to be present to celebrate friends and family. Not being present sends the message that we don't care about what they're experiencing at that moment. There are times to place our desires and priorities on a back burner in order that others can feel our appreciation. This could easily have been one of those times. Doubtless, the high-strung nature of Raphael might make him appear just a bit less lovable, and perhaps those around him would naturally feel less inclined to show their support.

The need to control can cost us many things: love, connection, peace, harmony, and relationships. These behaviors tend to slow their forward progress. People shut down when we force our intentions upon them. This quality is a repellant that sends a message that our opinion is more important than theirs.

Fear of Losing Control

Oftentimes, our actions are the result of trying to cover our unease. An inner voice tells us, "If I don't handle this, I'm going to spin out of control." This feeling is a good indication of a deeper story about what's really going on. It's our responsibility to see what truths its revealing.

When we don't get our way and are forced to sit with our truths, we may experience a great deal of frustration and annoyance. Raphael's frustration actually resulted from his inability to manage his discomfort. By not openly addressing what really bothers or upsets us, we might feel the need to control the environment. Raphael's commitment to keeping up the pace of the group prevents him from looking at his anxieties, which are the result of multiple issues. By ignoring his anxiety, he gives the false impression that everything is OK. Raphael controls the environment at every opportunity so that he won't have to look at his issues. Unfortunately, what we attempt to control ends up controlling us.

Life in Crisis - Todd loves Lucy?

Event:

Todd and Lucy have been dating in Los Angeles for several months. Lucy is an actress, trying to get a big break. Todd is a social media influencer and brand ambassador. In other words, he takes lots of pictures to post on Instagram! On the surface they seem to have a good relationship. They're consistent, see each other on a regular basis, and things between them had been just fine. What Lucy doesn't know, is that Todd's last girlfriend left him for a film producer she met at a movie premiere they were attending last year. Lately, Todd is concerned with every move Lucy makes and where she goes when he is not around. He doesn't want her looking at other guys and doesn't want them looking at her. In the past month, Todd embarrassed her by confronting a guy she was innocently talking to at a party. She was shocked and concerned. Her faith in the relationship is now waning. What's wrong Todd?

Synopsis:

Todd has anxiety of Lucy leaving him like his last relationship and manages his fears by attempting to control her. In his mind, Todd has a very good reason for his behavior. By deciding where they eat, where they go out and where they drink, he is managing who sees her and who she sees. Lately, Lucy has had enough of this and wants distance from Todd. His controlling behavior virtually guarantees he will lose her, and this time it won't be because of another guy, but because of himself.

The anxiety, fear, or worry that we're trying to manage could lead us to control. Fortunately, we have the power to eliminate this angst, and in so doing, diminish these tendencies. Bossing others around sets us up for a life of conflict and loneliness.

The Pain of Control

Being controlled generates pain, which often manifests as anger, discomfort, or frustration. We all desire freedom and empowerment and detest being forced against our will. Not wanting to be told what to do means we'll resent being controlled at all costs. When others think they know what's best for us, we often react with hostility and anger. It's as if they assume that we don't know how to take care of ourselves.

There are many things controlling people aren't saying out loud, but are communicating through their actions: insecurity, instability, and discomfort. They must be inherently unhappy because their happiness is contingent upon the compliance of others. Their tension is evident because they are heavily invested in getting their way or risk falling apart. Obviously, control comes at a great cost. The perceived reward must be significant to pay such a price.

KEY PAIN POINTS OF CONTROLLING PEOPLE

- They exhibit a high degree of emotional chaos when they're not in control. This inevitably drives people away.
- A common characteristic is exhibiting a dictatorial nature. This creates either resentful compliance or resistance.
- They send the message that other's opinions don't matter. People stop participating in conversations which lead to ineffective and disconnected relationships.
- Their underlying belief is that they know best. This results in a competitive dynamic that translates into unhealthy and contentious relationships.
- They often attempt to force their intentions on an individual or a group. Most often, people will reject or resist forced intention and direct themselves in the opposite way.

Language of Controlling People

"We're doing it my way. Get behind me and follow."

"When I'm not in control, I'm out of control."

"I can't handle myself, so I'm going to control something else."

CHAPTER 7

YOU DON'T ALWAYS GET WHAT YOU EXPECT

"If you expect nothing from somebody you are never disappointed." - Sylvia Plath

Understanding Demands

Unhealthy demands and expectations are non-negotiable rules or laws that we apply to anything or anyone. Expectations often come with emotional investments in a desired outcome. It is unhealthy to impede another person's ability to be freely expressed.

When we don't get what we want, this can lead to chaos, unhappiness, upset, or being let down. When we do get what we demand, the best outcome is only short-term satisfaction. This might also cause others a great amount of upset if they're being coerced to act against their will. They may acquiesce to our expectations, simply to retain a peaceful relationship, but not necessarily because they are in agreement. We can wreak havoc on others when making demands. These selfish behaviors most often come back to haunt us.

Demands vs. Expectations

There is a fundamental difference between demands and expectations. Demands are spoken, while expectations are inferred. When an expectation is communicated, it becomes a demand. When someone says, "I expect you to do x, y, or z," that is nothing more than a dressed-up demand. There is an obvious aspect of manipulation in both of them.

The degree of emotional investment we have in an expectation or demand, determines the amount of upset we experience when it's not met. When this happens, we often look for someone or something to hold accountable. It certainly won't be us, so the search is on!

Demands can be a learned character trait and we may believe that we're entitled to them. The idea that this is normal behavior could have been communicated from our families, parents, professors and friends. What's "normal" doesn't always equate to what's healthy. Happiness is seldom a by-product of living such a life.

When our happiness is dependent upon outside circumstances being met, we cannot experience inner peace. As our demands are met, the best we can experience is ego satisfaction, which is temporary. The ego must be continuously satisfied at every twist and turn to maintain the good feeling it receives. We deceive ourselves into believing that this is happiness, when in reality, it is created internally. Don't mistake feeling good about something with experiencing true joy. We often misidentify happiness with things that satisfy our ego.

An expectation is when a girlfriend expects her boyfriend to take her out on Valentine's Day. This sense of entitlement doesn't allow the boyfriend to earn brownie points for fulfilling an expectation. The best he can do is stay out of the proverbial dog-house.

When someone needs their expectation to be met to feel OK, it can come across as needy. Turning over our personal power to someone else and asking them to make us feel good is a recipe for disaster. When we rely on the actions of others, we reinforce the message that we can't take care of ourselves. We're good at identifying what we want and need from others but haven't studied ourselves with the same intensity. We may be excellent at creating demands and expectations, but the key is to be self-sufficient.

Life in Crisis - Bill and Clark's excellent un-adventure

Event:
Bill and Clark live in Laguna Beach and have decided to work on a solar start-up. They've been great friends for 3 years, but they've never worked together. Bill, 47, lives alone and has a lot of free time on his hands. Clark, 31, has a roommate and they are always going out on the town. Bill is a conscientious guy, who is serious and methodical. When he is engaged with a project he invests 100% of his energy. He became a stock investor and taught himself how to trade stocks by watching YouTube videos and reading books. This entrepreneurial venture is beyond the scope of their current work. At first, they worked together as a team, but Bill started taking on more of the project demands. As time passed, Bill committed more energy into the project, working deep into the night. Their contributions started to become unbalanced. Bill was building up resentment toward Clark. One night, Clark was out at a sports bar with his roommate when his phone was beeping with text after text from Bill. The texts challenged Clark to complete his responsibilities for the project by the next day. Clark was never in agreement with this. After ignoring 4 texts from Bill,

the final text came through... "I see you're not interested in this, maybe I should look for another partner." Clark slapped his forehead and winced.

Synopsis:
Bill had expectations that weren't being met and Clark was not in agreement. Bill expected him to contribute to the project in a manner that had never been discussed. Then he became resentful and angry when Clark wasn't contributing at the same commitment level. Bill has too much time on his hands and Clark has too little. This is workable, but Bill must communicate his wants and needs more clearly and get a buy-in from Clark rather than simply making demands without consent. Without communication, Bill and Clark can expect this project to be an epic fail!

Reflections:
Sometimes in life it makes sense to have expectations. At work, we are expected to take care of our responsibilities. At home, we might be expected to take out the trash and feed the family. Having them is not always the problem. It only becomes an issue if we become upset when they are not met. It's OK to have an expectation, if we do not allow it to dictate our emotional wellness. If we consistently get upset when things don't go our way, we set ourselves up for a life of torture. Life doesn't always happen the way we want, but if we remain flexible and adaptable, we can minimize our distress and maximize our inner-peace.

Having expectations is similar to believing what we think "should" happen. They become unhealthy when they interfere with someone else's ability to act freely. We are setting ourselves up for unnecessary conflict whenever we place our expectations on others. People have free-will and have the ability to respond however they wish. Just because we have a narrowly defined field of vision, doesn't mean they must acquiesce and follow. The rules and regulations that we have for ourselves don't necessarily work for others and they may not even work for us. We remain trapped for as long as we choose to have demands and expectations. To develop productive relationships with people, we must stop manipulating and start honoring them.

Expectations can create a false sense of emotional security. We might feel secure anticipating what is going to happen next. When the results don't match our expectations, we might experience anger or upset. By demanding an outcome, we minimize relationships, relegating them to nothing more than robot status. As such, their actions become more like conditioned responses; less authentic and vibrant.

Life in Crisis – Tan lines and drama

Event:
Mitch works retail in Ft. Lauderdale and is very busy throughout the day. He has been with the same girlfriend for the past year and things are going well. As a manager, Mitch is often called in at the last minute and is expected to fill in when there's a personnel issue. Zane is an entrepreneur and has flexible free-time throughout the day. He's always at the gym and likes to tan at Las Olas beach. Mitch and Zane have been best friends for 5 years. Mitch gets a kick out of Zane's eccentric qualities and appreciates their differences as much as their similarities. Zane has an active imagination, as well as social life. He often reports to Mitch about his crazy dates and the guys he meets. Mitch is happy to listen and offer his thoughts.

Zane recently met a guy he really liked and had gone on a few dates. He felt like this was THE ONE! In the middle of lunch one day, the guy ended up walking out abruptly. Zane called and texted Mitch about the whole thing, but on that day, Mitch was working the 6:00 a.m. – 4:00 p.m. shift. After work, he went to see a movie with his girlfriend. Mitch replied to Zane's text but not his call. They spoke the next day and Zane was upset that his call wasn't returned the prior day. His message was clear that something important had happened. Based on a history of their relationship, he expected that Mitch would promptly return his call. When that didn't happen, he became upset.

Synopsis:

Zane needed Mitch to behave in a way that fell in line with his expectations so that he could feel secure and appreciated. His expectations unknowingly gave Mitch limited options on how to behave. Zane is entitled to communicating his feelings and there is nothing wrong with wanting Mitch to return his calls promptly. It only became unhealthy when the request turned into a demand that was not agreed upon. Zane's expectations created an unhappy experience for him, while Mitch was completely unaware. He's an innocent bystander who got pulled into a drama whirlwind. Zane failed to inform him of their unwritten contract that they would always behave a certain way with each other. His intense attachments blinded him from the truth that Mitch does care about him. Zane only feels cared for when friends behave a certain way. When he didn't receive that experience from Mitch, it bothered him. Zane is unaware that Mitch treats all his good friends in the same manner and isn't singling him out. Huge miss, Zane! Whoever is demanding will inevitably suffer one way or another.

We're not Mind-Readers

It is crazy-making to get upset when someone doesn't act according to our wishes, and they had no idea of them in the first place. Even if they know what we expect, it's audacious to demand of them to march in line with our every wish. We can't apply our rules and regulations to everyone else. They are free to behave however they wish and we are free to respond accordingly.

Life in Crisis – Three's a crowd?

Event:
Brad and Mary live in St. Louis and have been dating for 2 years. They have an ongoing, one-sided discussion regarding Brad's desire to constantly hang out with his college buddies. They all attended Washington University and stayed connected over the years. Mary doesn't like that Brad lives with his college best friends. They're all around 30 years old, play video games, cards and generally enjoy each other's company. Mary lives alone. Brad wishes she would agree to spend time with the entire group. Mary would rather spend time alone with Brad. One night, they had planned a date but one of Brad's good friends from college rolled into town. Brad suggested that they make it a three-some and all hang out. Mary hit the ceiling, complaining to Brad about the little amount of one-on-one time they spend together. Brad couldn't figure out why that's such a big deal. Their relationship is on the rocks. Mary wonders, will Brad ever grow up? Brad wonders, "will Mary ever be willing to be part of the group?"

Synopsis:
Brad expects Mary to joyously be a part of his group of friends. Mary expects Brad to grow up, make a commitment to her and honor her desire for one-on-one time. Each has their own

expectation of how the relationship should look and they can't seem to get on the same page. These expectations are crippling their bond. Brad cannot in any way understand, nor does he try to understand Mary. He expects everyone should want the same things as he. Thinking that way refutes her wishes. He doesn't see the remote possibility of a different point of view. To Brad, everyone should want to hang out with their friends and make it a party. When he doesn't get compliance, he gets frustrated and distances himself from Mary. Brad wants to set the standard for how the relationship works and he expects his girlfriend to think as he does. Brad's expectations create a sense of entitlement. This arrogant, narrow-minded view is what will cause him to suffer and Mary to distance herself.

Reflections:
This might also happen in the reverse, where Mary demands that Brad not hang out with his friends and only spend time with her. In some relationships, this is the norm. This relationship will remain in gridlock until both parties relax their demands and expectations and engage in meaningful compromises.

Self-Centered Bias

To have expectations of others is like putting a leash around our own neck. As we limit their options, we place ourselves in a holding pattern, awaiting their compliance. Our emotional state is determined by the outcome of their actions. We literally hand over our well-being and are held hostage in the process. Inner peace is dependent on our ability to accept others as they are, and not on our ability to make demands. Our self-centered thinking is the problem, not their lack of compliance.

Life in Crisis- Lesley had a little lamb

Event:

Greg is 30 years old, soft-natured, easy-going and lives in Dallas. He's very compassionate, sensitive, and feels a little less masculine than other guys because of his gentle spirit. His girlfriend, Lesley, is a powerhouse attorney in a large litigation law firm. They met at a Tony Robbins breakthrough weekend, and Lesley was super impressed with Greg's wisdom and calm. She works 60-hour weeks, wears 3-inch heels, and is smartly attired in one of 20 different suits from Brooks Brothers that hangs in her closet. Lesley sits on two different volunteer boards and is a competitive marathon runner. Greg is a guitar teacher and a member of the local Buddhist temple. He wears beads and Nirvana T-shirts. He is vegetarian and leads meditation on Sundays at the Cosmic Cafe. He is planning to attend an ayahuasca ceremony in Peru in a few weeks.

Although Lesley finds Greg's wisdom and calm alluring, and the sex is great, she experiences him to be too compliant. He never argues with her or anyone else and she is sick of seeing the Ankh that hangs around his neck. She is very opinionated about his passive nature and has even asked him several times if he's gay. Her ex-boyfriend was a marine who didn't take attitude from anyone. Lesley found this to be very attractive. One night, Greg and Lesley were at a Torchy's Tacos restaurant, and a group of loud, young fraternity guys jumped ahead of them in line. Greg shrugged his shoulders, looked at Lesley and smiled, not thinking much of it. While standing in line, Lesley screamed about his nonchalant reaction, and reminded him that her ex wouldn't have let those obnoxious kids get away with it. She went on to point out that a dominant male wouldn't let that happen and that he shouldn't be so weak. The more peaceful and non-reactive Greg was, the angrier and tenser Lesley became. Greg was mortified and embarrassed of her reaction. He found her repulsive in that moment. Lesley associates passive nature with weakness. Is there a future for these love-birds?

Synopsis:
Lesley inhabits a world much different than Greg's. In her world, powerful people make things happen, running over anyone who gets in their way. She marches in step with society's expectations that men should behave a certain way and assert themselves as needed. She demands her boyfriend to see it the same way. Greg is annoyed by Lesley's constant questioning of his masculinity. Her expectations of how a man should behave, puts him on the spot and makes him feel like he's not enough for her. He's grown tired of this and even doubts his own masculinity at times because of her constant nagging. Greg doesn't want to live this way and is considering if they have irreconcilable differences. Lesley's expectations and demands that Greg behave a certain way, rob him of the freedom to be who he is and pushes the relationship to the brink of failure. It's clear that Lesley's expectations dictate and damage the quality of her intimate relationships. That ayahuasca ceremony can't come quickly enough for Greg! Note to Lesley - he's been telling you who he is since you met. If you can't accept it, maybe it's time to move on and not try to change him!

From Prison to Freedom

We are naturally drawn to people who encourage us to be ourselves. That type of freedom exists only when we can make our own choices. When we force our rules and standards on people who don't want them, we diminish the possibility for real connection. Forcing another person to comply with our self-centered demands can only leave them feeling manipulated and played.

There is no one, right way to live. There are only the experiences we choose for ourselves. If it works for us, then we can keep having it. If not, we can stop. However, we can't demand anything from anyone else. The healthy choice is always to state our desires, accept others where they are, and to stay true to ourselves.

KEY PAIN POINTS OF DEMANDS

AND EXPECTATIONS

- There is no sense of joy when someone is denied free choice. It becomes a hollow victory when anyone acts according to another's demands.
- Expectations create a "mind-reader" mentality and may not be met because people can't read your mind.
- The expected outcome is everything. Happiness is contingent upon that outcome being met. We end up pushing everyone away and they walk on egg-shells in our company.
- Demands and expectations elicit people-pleasing behaviors. People-pleasers fall in line in ways that support the expectations of others. Losing themselves, they become a supporting actor in someone else's story.

Language of Demands and Expectations

"Everything will be OK as long as it happens the way I want."

"It's my way or the highway!"

CHAPTER 8

WHEN I JUDGE YOU, I JUDGE ME

"The ability to observe without evaluating is the highest form of intelligence." - Jiddu Krishnamurti

The Nature of Judgment

When we judge others, we often judge ourselves on the same issue. This behavior keeps us from experiencing compassion and reveals our character defects. Low self-esteem can also lead us to judge because in so doing, we can feel better or more important. If we didn't already suffer from a poor self image, why would we feel the need to assert ourselves as better than someone else? Ignorance, or lack of awareness of another person's situation, makes them easier targets for criticism. Awareness of another's situation combined with empathy, creates the context for compassion.

Tunnel vision means seeing things only one way. If it doesn't fit our frame of reference, we might reject or condemn it. Being exposed to different environments can contribute to an accepting nature. The more we understand someone's story, the more empathy we can have for them.

Why We Judge

Judgment is an act of bringing others down to our level of unhappiness. This necessitates either an outside or inside solution. Searching within, we take responsibility for our discomfort. This might look like taking inventory of how our actions or non-actions cause our own misery. We can understand the role we have played in creating unhappiness and are now able to change our lives.

Looking outside ourselves for a solution, others become potential whipping dogs. When we're blind to the role we've played in creating our upset, or refuse to look at it, then we must externalize our pain by looking at others for comparison. As we compare ourselves, we see them as either "better than" or "less than."

When we perceive someone as "better than," we must knock them down. In this way we even the playing field and make ourselves feel better. Envy also can be a function of seeing someone higher than ourselves. This can act as a motivator to knock them down a peg. We attempt to resolve our unhappiness through someone else's demise. Our incentive to diminish them causes us to judge. In so doing, we perceive that somehow, we've evened the score.

Seeing someone as "less than," we can assume a superior mentality. This results in adopting a critical nature. Knocking someone down legitimizes our sense of authority. This power trip inevitably leads to judgment. Making someone else wrong makes us feel right and powerful. We want to be right because when we are wrong we feel badly about ourselves, and our ego is hurt. To feel better, we may judge so that we can feel competent, and therefore, secure. Failure to work on our issues sets us up for a life of blame, judgment and disaster.

What Judgment Reveals

Judging reveals far more about the person enacting it than it does about the victim. If we could feel the pain we inflict onto others, we might develop empathy that would stop our hurtful behavior in its tracks. We ultimately hurt ourselves when we put others down because it reinforces a self-judgmental nature that always finds its way home.

Although we may not realize at the time, what we do to others, we also do to ourselves. If it is our instinct to scrutinize others under a microscope, it may be because we have that same instinct to scrutinize ourselves. When we're unsatisfied, we often take it out on someone else. By bashing, we make them wrong and "less than." In comparison, we are now able to feel better. As such, we've used them as a tool to prop up our low self-esteem.

We judge to manage our own insecurities or big egos, but ultimately feel worse about ourselves in the long run. We make the world a less enjoyable and safe place each time we criticize someone. Further, we limit the love that we can receive because those judged won't feel the safety to be authentic in our company. In our attempts to prop ourselves up, we actually end up pushing others away.

Life in Crisis - The ultimate fashion police

Event:
Alexis was born into a well-to-do family and attended a private boarding school in Virginia. The girls drive the latest luxury imports and have their hair pulled in beautifully appointed pony-tails. Often, there is an air about them, and some take on fake accents and others throw their hands in the air with dramatic gestures to draw attention to themselves.

Today, Alexis is a senior sorority member and is the self-proclaimed fashion police of the Delta Delta Delta Chapter at the University of Florida. She criticizes her sorority sisters as much as possible. She often talks badly about her friends behind their backs. She judges the hair, make-up, and nails of her sisters. She keeps up with the latest Vogue, Cosmo, and People magazine issues. Consumed with pop culture, snap-chat, and her 150,000 Instagram followers, Alexis proudly posts her latest nail polish and lipstick colors as an opinion leader.

To her, that might be all well and good, but none of her sorority sisters think she's entertaining or interesting. To them, she is exhausting and judgmental. At the last sorority meeting Alexis took a Burger King Crown and placed it on the heaviest sorority member and declared she was the queen of fast food. This was the last straw and now there is a vote scheduled by the Chapter deciding whether to keep or boot her. When is enough, enough?

Synopsis:
Alexis really believes she is better than everyone else! Each time she exhibits judgmental behavior, her girlfriends don't want to be around her. When Alexis dishes on Judy's new look to Mary, that critique causes trust issues because who's to say when Mary will be subjected to her judgmental nature? What this says about Alexis is that she will most likely do this to everyone. Because of her judgments, Alexis's sorority sisters never allow themselves to be vulnerable and are always on guard. Alexis creates an environment where everyone around her walks on eggshells. Most feel the need to rush out and read the latest Cosmo magazine and make sure they have the right look before seeing her. We only connect with people authentically when we can be our vulnerable, true selves. When under the microscope of judgment, her sisters don't feel free to

be themselves. This leads them to withdraw and it ultimately isolates Alexis. Now she faces possible expulsion from her sorority. She must be exhausted trying to live up to her own standards as well! It's a heavy burden.

The Costs of Judgment

By now we understand how judgment pushes people out of our lives. This produces an environment where it feels like it's not safe to be ourselves. We guard our most intimate aspects when threatened by a potential attack. To protect ourselves, we block access to our hearts. This happens because we lack the capacity to develop deep relationships. Only when we feel accepted can we be authentic. Vulnerability and trust are at the core of any meaningful relationship. True equanimity can be experienced when nobody's head is higher or lower than our own.

To judge is to decide that something or someone is right or wrong. The problem with "right or wrong" thinking is that it delivers a winner and a loser. This zero-sum game causes a great deal of concern. If someone must be wrong in order for us to be right, we know we are being led by judgment, which ultimately results in two losers and no winners.

Life in Crisis - The point about pointing fingers

Event:
Neil is a computer nerd who attends Colorado University. He doesn't mean anyone any harm, he just causes it. He comes from a large family with six children and was often not heard throughout his childhood. He's a soft-natured guy for the most part, until you get him talking about politics or any other subject about which he's passionate. Conversing about Starcraft or Guild Wars really gets him going. He has a history of making people wrong when he is the expert on the subject.

He spends countless hours ransacking internet websites for information that nobody else would know so that he can win every debate. Neil follows thought-leaders, bloggers, and mainstream media to stay current. He has a knack for turning casual conversations into a debate. As such, Neil regards everyone else's opinion as wrong, and his as right. It wouldn't be out of character for him to blurt out, "that's ridiculous" in response to others' comments. At his core, Neil thinks he's superior to everyone else and they're just idiots who don't deserve to be heard.

One night while at dinner with three friends in Boulder, a benign dialogue started. Within 5 minutes, he was pointing his finger and began to monopolize the conversation. Neil became so intense, that he had no interest in listening to anyone else. In fact, the conversation never really mattered. He only cared about making everyone else wrong. The other participants stared in horror as he made a spectacle of himself. Neil emphatically stated his position, completely disregarding everyone else and pointing at them to assert his dominance. Almost like a circus act, he exhibited bizarre behavior, without being aware of it. To him, it was just a normal night. He left feeling fantastic. Everyone else was drained and disgusted.

Synopsis:
Those in Neil's company felt diminished, disregarded, and unimportant. Being committed to being right means everyone else must be wrong. There are people who view conversations as debates. Neil was challenging everyone at the table. What began as friendly chatter, ended up as a debate that nobody else wanted. Those who were at dinner that night will think twice about the next time they're invited to dinner with Neil. Nobody wins when someone positions things as right and wrong; there is only the experience of judging and being judged. Neither of these is desirable. The Neil's of the world

aren't particularly pleasant company. Neil is ruled by his fear of not being noticed or being wrong. A lifetime of having no voice means that today, he must exert his opinion without boundaries and disregards everyone else's. The tragedy is that while he gets his worth from voicing his opinion, he alienates everyone and makes no friends in the process.

Judgment and the Food Chain

When we make someone wrong, we make ourselves right. The sense of superiority this instills can be intoxicating. The need to be smarter or better is related to personal insecurities. Thus, it's safe to say that our need to be right mirrors our need to feel secure. While insecure, we exhibit a comparative predisposition. We might assess how we measure up to others and how they measure up to us. If we score on the low end of our imaginary scale, we might feel badly about ourselves. Since we don't want to be outranked, we begin to believe that stepping on others is a way to increase our value. As we reach the top of the food chain, we can look down to see how many people had to fall so that we could rise. Is the view from the top really as attractive as we thought it would be?

We are embroiled in competition when we approach things in a comparative manner. The problem with being concerned with a food chain is that the struggle never ends and there is always someone vying to improve their position. We will either be offensive or defensive in the game. We may need to take an offensive strategy, which would mean judging others to improve our position on the board.

At the core of judgments is the need to be right, which contains a "better than" component. We can't judge, unless we're comparing. I can only be better if you're worse. I can only be right if you're wrong. I can only be lower, if you're higher.

Life in Chaos – Ben and Jerry's melt down

Event:
Ben is a 40-year-old real-estate professional, living in Boston. He is in perfect shape, always has great hair, and meticulous manicures. His office is impeccable. The walls contain awards and certificates, as a statement of his position in the company and his accomplishments. His office is aromatic and everything on his desk is arranged. Ben has mastered the experience of creating aesthetic perfection. Jerry is an easy-going 23-year-old and a recent graduate of Boston College. He enjoys casual conversations with friends and likes to dress comfortably. He loves to prop up his Allbirds shoes on the desk while he negotiates deals. He's always smiling, happy-go-lucky and is trying to build a reputation in the company. He is the low man on the totem pole and hopes to have Ben's status one day. Ben is Jerry's executive mentor at Top Shelf Realty. Ben often casts disapproving glances toward Jerry in the hallway. One day, Jerry stopped by his office unexpectedly while Ben was on the phone. He motioned to Jerry to have a seat while he completed the call. As he finished, he eyed Jerry up and down with a disapproving look on his face. After he hung up, he unleashed on Jerry. "When was your last hair-cut and how much did it cost? Your clothes, do you even wash them?" He continued, "Don't you think it's time for a make-over? Who in this town will take you seriously with that get-up?" Ben doesn't mean to be rude, he just is. Jerry is becoming increasingly frustrated with this arrangement.

Synopsis:
To Ben, he thinks he's helping Jerry. He's just being honest. The thing is, Jerry didn't ask him for that feedback and Jerry's doing just fine without it. Ben has a way of making others feel insignificant and less than. Jerry didn't see the abuse coming, but he got shamed. When Jerry received Ben's comments, it

discouraged him and made him feel like it's not OK to have his own professional style. How can anyone feel secure when they feel judged? For someone to truly let loose and comfortably be their authentic self, they must feel safe. When we feel free to be self-expressed, there is no fear of being made wrong. When we judge, those around us never feel totally safe being themselves. In a work environment, it's important to remember that everyone has their own style, just like outside of work. What works for one person might not work for another. It's important to honor the unique qualities and characteristics of each individual.

Professionally, it's very easy to engage in this behavior. Higher ranking status within organizations often creates the sense of entitlement to judge those lower ranking. The desire for upward mobility makes junior associates more susceptible to the effects of professional criticism. Placing senior executives on a pedestal can make us feel less-than. It is incumbent upon us not to allow their opinions to diminish our personal dignity. Simply because someone outranks us does not give them the power to negatively affect our self-esteem.

Your Life, Your Rules

Judgment causes us to push people away. Nobody wants to be judged, nor do they give us the authority. It is typically self-appointed and done so at the cost of virtually every relationship. Even when trying to assist someone with issues of personal growth, any unsolicited advice can easily be construed as judgment. It's a very grey area to assume we know what's best for anyone. We might know what works for us (even that might be debatable) but don't always know what's best for another. Therefore, we must be cautious when offering unsolicited counsel. A good rule of thumb is to exercise caution when offering constructive feedback if nobody's asked for it.

KEY PAIN POINTS OF JUDGMENT

• Judgmental people hurt themselves when judging others. This virtually guarantees misery and lack of true connectedness.

• This nature can stem from a position of competitiveness. This causes others to shut-down or depart, which means the "victor" celebrates in loneliness or isolation.

• No one ever wins in a world of right and wrong. It sets up a constant tug of war that makes people avoid us.

• A professional aspect of judging is the colleague who makes everyone else wrong. This disempowers others within the organization.

• Seniority or higher rank within a company does not mean that it's open season on those lower ranking. It's the responsibility of the person judged to protect their personal dignity.

Language of Judgment

"I'm right and you're wrong."

"I'm OK, and you're not OK."

CHAPTER 9

MEANING-MAKING GONE WRONG

"There is nothing either good or bad, but thinking makes it so." - William Shakespeare

Why We Make Meaning

Meaning-making is the process of how we make sense of events, circumstances, or people. It has the quality of creating context where there wasn't any before. It is a human characteristic and is inherent to our nature. It frames and defines our world views and structures our lives.

We do this so that we can define our experiences with certainty. Meanings deliver clear definitions that we can readily understand. A large degree of this activity is learned from our peers, family, and social interactions. We decide what things mean from our personal experiences and frames of reference. A pre-disposition toward negative meaning making delivers anger, upset, or disappointment.

Meaning provides a concrete definition that we need to feel secure. When something makes sense to us, we can feel comfortable and grounded. It's possible to change our fundamental programming of how we interpret events by assuming the power and responsibility to positively articulate our experiences.

The associations that we form in life will either add to or take away from our happiness. How we define what is happening affects how we feel about ourselves. When we choose empowering meanings, we feel better. It is when we assume negative ones, that we misinterpret, blame, and make ourselves a victim or persecutor. The definitions we choose shape our inner and outer realities. Thus, it is critical that we take ownership of this process.

Life in Crisis – MacArthur's Park is melting in the dark

Event:
Jen is a 37-year-old divorced art dealer in Los Gatos and has a 4-year-old daughter. Tom is 34, and a successful internet entrepreneur. He is committed to financial growth and has built a company of 25 employees. Six months ago, Tom broke off a 3-year engagement because his fiancé became too needy. He is an art collector and met Jen at an art gallery in San Francisco and began dating her soon after. They were walking arm in arm through MacArthur Park one cool September evening. Tom was enjoying the sights and sounds of people doing yoga, kids playing and dogs barking. He was in a state of complete observation and personal bliss. He had closed a big deal earlier that day and was beaming. Jen had spoken to her Mother earlier that day and it put her in a foul mood. Tom bumped into one of his employees and had a 10-minute conversation with her about work. After that conversation, they began to walk home. Feeling neglected, Jen decided to give Tom the silent treatment. Instead of addressing Tom directly, Jen's anger took on a passive-aggressive role. Tom suggested that they go to a great new restaurant in Union Square, and she replied, "I think I just want to go home." Tom couldn't

understand what was wrong, but he probably wasn't going to find out that night. All he knew was that something wasn't right. As Jen left to go home, he watched her and wondered, "What the heck just happened?"

Synopsis:
Jen could make a sunny day dark. Based on her failed marriage, she has insecurities about new guys she is dating. She has the capacity to take anything and everything her boyfriend does, and make it mean something negative – and boy, does she! The sad thing is that she construes meaning that brings her pain and suffering. When Tom stopped to speak with his employee, Jen made it mean that he would rather speak to someone else rather than spend time talking with her. She felt that Tom wasn't focusing attention on her. Unfortunately, a lot of Jen's meaning-making causes her deep pain. Seldom does she make meaning that gives her joy. Instead of enjoying the sunny day with her man, she chose to create an overcast day filled with negative thoughts. Tom was shocked when he witnessed her behavior, which could easily cause him to second guess their relationship. Jen will sabotage her relationship with Tom until she stops making negative meaning and sees the love that is already there. Jen misinterpreted the events because she felt insecure. This way of looking at things kept her from enjoying a wonderful day out with Tom.

Much of what we feel is determined by what we make things mean. If we have enough evidence, we can believe anything. There is always plenty of information to support multiple views of the same situation. The question then becomes, what evidence are we committed to looking for? Are we committed to searching for evidence that causes us pain, or are we committed to searching for evidence that promotes joy? Both options are available. The one in which we invest our thoughts, delivers our reality.

The Roots of Negative Meanings

Since we know that negative meaning-making typically results in pain and misery, it's worth asking the question, "why would anyone choose it?" History produces the context for behavioral patterns, which we unconsciously follow. These patterns are usually learned from generations in our families. Sometimes we develop them on our own and they continue operating over and over again. Being unhappy or depressed provides fertile conditions to view events in a negative light which further compounds our misery.

We can make negative meaning out of a situation and refuse to see it any other way because we get to be right. We may have evidence that supports a contrary point of view, but choose being right and miserable, over peace and happiness.

Although it often causes suffering, we often continue doing the same things over and over again because they're familiar. Living from our comfort zones, we learn to live with upset because change would require more effort than we are willing to expend.

Life in Crisis – The lonely man and his neighbor

Event:
Grant is 60 years old and lives in an apartment building in Miami that was built with poor construction. He is a copy-writer and spends most of his time working from home. He is creative and highly sensitive to his surroundings. It's easy to hear anyone living above him or next door. Although he is sensitive to noise, he chose to live downstairs for convenience. Now, he is convinced that the people who live above him are out to get him. They moved in a few weeks ago and have a dog that he will occasionally hear barking. Further, when they are

home, he hears them making a commotion and is convinced that the sound increases when he is active in the apartment. The amazing thing is, Grant has already experienced 3 different tenants living above him, and they all seem to have something in common – they're all trying to make his life miserable by willfully creating discord. Grant is convinced beyond a shadow of a doubt that every time he hears a footstep upstairs, it's a response to something he's done, or a statement of their dissatisfaction with him. He is miserable and at wit's end. He's thinking of all his options, including moving.

Synopsis:

Grant makes meaning of every single thing he hears and lives in constant vigilance, waiting for the next sound. It's always personal to him. It can never simply be that the upstairs neighbor dropped a shoe. It's that they're trying to get at him for something he's done or something he's going to do.

In Grant's world, this is reality. It is one of loneliness and sadness. His sense of self is confirmed by the actions of the upstairs neighbor. He makes everything mean that the world is against him. A life of loss has resulted in this mental and emotional framework for Grant. Is anybody listening? If Grant could reframe his experience, he would find peace of mind.

Toxic Self-Talk

We must assume responsibility for our worldview. It's easy to fall into the trap of seeing everything working against us and we must guard against this tendency when things are going "wrong." The effects of thinking this way are far-reaching and debilitating. Living from this toxic headset, we begin to invent stories that a storm is brewing. The more self-absorbed we are, the more powerful the effects. Boredom and loneliness are fertile ground for negative thoughts to flourish.

Life in Crisis – Will the real Ricky please stand up?

Event:

Ricky always knew he liked men and didn't have a problem with that at all. He came out at the age of 20 at Iowa State University but struggled to find other gay friends on campus. Ricky recently graduated from college and was living in Chicago. As Ricky began to make new friends, he found himself surrounded by 25-35-year-old gay men. He began to experience social interaction in a gay community for the first time. Sunday brunch, cruising guys, shopping on Michigan Ave., competition for wittiness, and of course, extravagant dinner parties became his world. Ricky felt he had to participate in all these shenanigans to have gay friends, even though he didn't really enjoy most of the activities. The thing is, Ricky was a simple guy from a small Midwestern town, who just wanted to hang out with some friends and enjoy life. Hanging out at home, watching National Geographic, and playing board games would have been the preferred experience. The more Ricky moved away from that, the unhappier he became. Does having friends mean that he must give up a part of himself to fit in and get along with the group?

Synopsis:

As Ricky surrounded himself with new friends, he found himself changing. He made being gay mean that it wasn't O.K. for him to want the things he wanted. He equated being gay with certain expected social norms. Even though it wasn't authentic to his nature, he acted as he felt he should. All he really wanted was a quiet night with close friends. Ricky felt that being part of a group meant that he had to behave a certain way to be accepted. Behaving that way did not bring Ricky happiness. He believed that friendships came with a list of rules on how to behave. In order to be a part of the community, he thought he had to act like everyone else. No one told him that it was mandatory. He conceived that idea for himself and subjected himself to what he perceived as the accepted norm. The sense we make of our environment has the power to alter our reality

Reflections:
This is a common challenge to anyone who feels that they must change a part of themselves to fit into a crowd or group. It's always important to ask ourselves, "Am I trying to be someone I'm not in order to fit in?"

Attention and Focus

What we focus on expands, so it's vitally important to pay attention to the meaning we attribute to events or situations. If our focus is undirected, our emotions might end up in places we don't desire. When filtering events we might ask ourselves, "What would I like to make this mean?" Interpreting events in a manner that benefits us would be far more empowering than allowing them to upset us.

Life in Crisis – Ding-dong the witch is dead

Event:
Renee views herself on a fast track to success. At 28, she worked at a small ad agency in Atlanta as the Marketing Director. Three days out of the week, she would show up late and would consistently leave early. She would throw her subordinates under the bus at every opportunity. It was common to overhear her shouting at someone in her office. Management questioned her commitment to the job and her abilities, delivering several warnings. The day ultimately came when Renee was fired. She had never been fired from anything in her life and had a history of running organizations. In some people's eyes, the company waited far too long. In Renee's eyes, she was unfairly targeted. She told everyone that management

was against her from the start and she felt singled out for mistreatment. Renee's version of events became the material of myths and fables.

Synopsis:
With bills to pay and a reputation to uphold, Renee struggled with what the firing meant. Unable to handle its severity, Renee invented a story that wasn't real. In effect, she told herself many lies so that she could handle the firing and ease the pain. First, management was against her and secondly, she was targeted because she was a woman. Her boss was stupid, and her colleagues were ineffective. These lies became her truths. The only way she could make it through this experience, was to make the firing mean something it didn't. Not being able to handle the truth, Renee is forever committed to self-deception as a coping mechanism. Some people alter their reality by telling themselves a story to protect their image. Without doing this, Renee would be left to face the painful truth of who she's been. Bottom line - nobody's going to miss Renee. Bye Bye!

Conclusion

Meaning-making is the art of defining experiences. We do this to make sense of life and reinforce our world view. We look for signs, and from them, generate meaning. For example, a hand gesture, a wink, or a look might give us an indication of how a relationship is progressing.

The foundations for making meaning can stem from family, society, churches, institutions, television, past experiences, and culture. We often find ourselves in relationship with others who make meaning in a similar manner. Meaning-making is influenced by our world view filter and reinforces it. Therefore, it is incumbent upon us to seize control of how we make meaning and understand its effects.

KEY PAIN POINTS OF NEGATIVE

MEANING-MAKING

- We are meaning-making machines that make things up that might not be reality. This can lead to our happiness or misery.
- We can unintentionally create emotional chaos from the meanings we make.
- When we choose meanings that don't serve us, we end up living by rules and standards that aren't satisfying.
- We deceive ourselves by twisting meanings to avoid difficult truths. In this way, we make meanings that allow us to feel OK.

Language of Negative Meaning-Making

"This means that, and so it is."

"I know they meant to disturb me because I'm upset!"

CHAPTER 10

LIMITING BELIEFS AND PERCEPTIONS

"Change the way you look at things and the things you look at change." - Wayne W. Dyer

Beliefs, Perceptions, Values and Identity

It's beneficial to contemplate what delivers happiness in life. Taking an inventory helps shine a light on whether we're positioned for happiness. It begins with how we see ourselves (our identity). Let's characterize the identity as the "I am" statement. It consists of both positive beliefs and limiting beliefs. These beliefs are comprised of values and perceptions.

Therefore, if we're not happy, we must carefully study our beliefs, perceptions and values. Values are what we consider important or relevant. Perceptions cause us to notice, focus on certain things, and look for validation in events. What we see is determined by what we value. If we value cleanliness, we will notice that quality everywhere. If we value peace and quiet, we will notice noise. When things don't line up with our values, we start operating from the left side of the Emotions Matrix (pg. 5).

There is a direct correlation between the value we place on our beliefs and our emotional responses. Some of our beliefs are neutral because we don't put a lot of emphasis into them. Therefore, not a lot of emotions are attached to them. On the other hand, some act as triggers and cause either highly positive or negative responses.

These beliefs and perceptions may have been hard-wired and are not readily changed. This is because most of them if not all, are backed by years of programming. With all that energy behind a belief, it takes courage to challenge it. There is however, a great deal of incentive to change the ones that deliver unhappiness. We can't be happy when our universe is spiraling downward. This is the outcome of allowing distorted thinking to control our lives.

Life in Crisis– Don't scroll, click LIKE

Event:
Miles was celebrating his 30th birthday in style. He entertained 20 of his closest friends in Manhattan with party favors. It was the party of the season in his mind. He excitedly posted the best group picture on Facebook and received over 500 likes. Tim is Miles' best friend who attended the party and is more of a serious type. He doesn't enjoy the silliness of Facebook and believes that tracking "likes" is a way for some people to feel better about themselves. The day after his birthday, Miles showed Tim the number of likes his post received. Tim responded with a sigh and rolled his eyes. Miles believed his best friend should've clicked "like" on the post. Tim couldn't believe they were having this conversation. He told Miles that this behavior seemed needy. Miles blew up. He blurted out, "If you can't count on your best friend to like your post, then who can you count on?" Tim shrugged his shoulders in confusion, still not understanding what this meant to Miles.

Synopsis:
Miles and Tim perceive the same event in completely different ways. Miles' posts on Facebook are a way for him to feel important. They're a numbers game that he intends to win. Tim has the opinion that Facebook is a waste of time. He is easy-going and doesn't get caught up in what other people think of him. The story that Miles tells himself about this event stems from his beliefs. His perceptions resulted in anger and resentment towards Tim, which serve as an indication that he is operating from a negative belief system. That anger and resentment will grow if Miles doesn't address the situation. So, we can see from this exchange how negative perceptions can damage our relationships.

The Interplay with Self-Esteem

Self-esteem is proportional to how we feel about our identity. When we honor our values, our self-esteem will increase. When we value things outside of ourselves, our self-esteem will experience ups and downs. When internal, we can experience greater stability and peace. How we feel on the inside trumps what we experience on the outside. Perceptions frame what we view as good or bad, making us happy or sad. Perceptions are a result of our values. Honoring our values, enhances our self-esteem.

Negative and distorted perceptions will always cause us to identify certain aspects of ourselves as "flawed." They can either support or destroy our self-esteem. Our sense of personal value is affected by what we think about ourselves. When we feel truly valuable, we can direct our perceptions and tune into the abundance that has always been in our lives. When we don't feel good about who we are, it will fuel limiting beliefs that focus our attention on inadequacies and cause upset.

Our experiences are filtered through self-esteem and influenced by our beliefs. These beliefs guide our perceptions and determine what we notice in ourselves and others. Do we notice our flaws or our strengths? The solution to many of our dilemmas is to focus on solving the root of the problem. Are we allowing limiting beliefs to influence our lives? When we become aware of our beliefs and how they contribute to our misery, it can motivate us to change. In so doing, we can alter our experience of life and enjoy more inner peace.

Life in Crisis – A portrait- somewhere in time

Event:

In Lisa's mind, she has a picture of herself. That picture was captured at 22 years of age. It is in black and white and she is standing in her wedding dress, alone at an altar on a foggy day in Seattle. This picture reflects the sadness of a girl who was stood up at her wedding. Although she is beautiful and 35 years old today, at 22, she decided she wasn't desirable. As Lisa went through grad school in Design and Fashion, she would shy away from the spotlight. She spent more and more time alone, working and studying so that she wouldn't have to socialize. She believes that she can't pick the right type of guys and doesn't trust herself. Lisa believes that the image of her at 22 is permanent. To her, she's stuck in time.

Synopsis:

Lisa suffers from a trauma that affected her sense of self many years ago. By reframing her wedding day in a manner that doesn't negatively affect her self-esteem, Lisa would free herself from inner pain and self-judgment. Shifting into the belief that being left behind at the altar wasn't her fault, would allow her to experience self-worth and freedom from a history of pain. Lisa took on the notion that she "should" be married and that would make her happy. She could let go of that societal expectation and liberate herself from feeling like a failure. In so doing, Lisa could replace the old black and white image of herself with one vibrant, in full color. She could enter back into life at any time of her choosing. Go Lisa, Go! The world's waiting for your re-entry! Perhaps we will see it, somewhere in time.

Altering our Point of View

A limited frame of reference will taint our experiences. We don't always know what's really going on because we don't have all the information. Perceptions are so uniquely ours, it isn't easy to see beyond them. There are multiple ways of viewing events, each equally valid. What we experience is influenced by what we notice and what we value. We mostly notice things that align with our beliefs and that matter.

We have the power to reframe and reshape experiences so that they don't debilitate and render us helpless. We must consider our perceptions and be willing to change them in order to get a desired outcome. So often, we perceive events from a narrow mind-set and it takes a different perspective to alter our relationship to them. Refusing to see it another way, we diminish the possibility for growth and transformation.

What other ways are possible for us to view an experience in order to generate a different emotional response? There are multiple ways to perceive any situation, so why would we choose to perceive something in a way that makes us feel bad? We interpret situations in ways that mirror how we feel about ourselves. For example, if I identify with being sad, my perception will be tuned into seeing things in a way that reflects that sadness. If I am happy, my perception will be tuned into seeing things in a manner that reflects that happiness. How we view the world determines the experiences we will have.

The ultimate lesson to learn about perceptions is that they can be altered. Some of us are committed to perceiving an event ONE WAY only. This rigid mind-set virtually locks us into a room of personal misery. If we're experiencing upset, the first order of business is to study ourselves. We must identify our recurring impulses if we desire to alter them.

Life in Crisis – The Monday through Thursday friend

Event:

Tanner is a 36-year-old divorced guy who lives in Phoenix. He was a very successful vice-president in corporate finance for the past five years. He left corporate America to become an entrepreneur and got divorced the same year. He loves Phoenix because of its youthful population and pretty people. Tanner is working hard on business plans for a new office park and is preparing spreadsheets for investors. His communication with the outside world is often limited. Finding single women his age isn't easy and he's most often attracted to younger women anyway. Tanner recently moved into a young adult community. Many of the residents seek out Tom's wisdom, asking him for advice, help and direction. Often, Tanner will spend his free-time advising them on their careers and relationships. He spends a great deal of his time throughout the week helping others. Often, Tanner takes them to dinner and picks up the tab. The problem is, on Friday nights, Tanner's phone goes radio-silent. Nobody contacts him from Friday nights until Monday mornings. He is increasingly depressed about the fact that his "friends" don't reach out to him unless they need something. He calls his mentor to discuss the situation because his lonely weekends are starting to affect his health and vitality.

Synopsis:

Tanner has a clear case of misperception. He perceives the people in his community as "friends." He confuses mentorship with friendship. He didn't make appropriate distinctions of how friendship and intimacy might look before investing his time. Tanner has a belief that says, "Hanging out with someone, giving them advice, and taking them to dinner, makes them my friend." This belief is uniquely his, not shared by those who surround and use him. Others can make the distinction between friendship and mentorship, but not Tanner. He will need a radical new way of perceiving friendship to alter his loneliness. We also know that the life of an entrepreneur can be lonely, and Tanner must distinguish between personal and professional relationships. He has relied on his abilities, wealth and wisdom to attract people whom he labeled as friends. He never felt that he was enough for someone to want to spend time with him. When he recognizes his worth and redefines his definition of friendship, Tanner will begin attracting love and relationships that make him happy. We see you, Tanner!

Beliefs, Actions and Reality

Our perceptions and beliefs create our realities. The stories we tell ourselves about what happened have more to do with what we believe, and how we perceive them than about what really transpired. Beliefs are like agreements we make with reality. One person's paradigm might not resonate with another's. Not only do we create our realities, but we also attract them based on our beliefs. We direct and channel our attention toward whatever feels "right." We spend a great deal of energy searching for evidence to support our positions. Our perceptions are tuned to notice things that confirm our beliefs.

Beliefs are basically inner convictions with deep roots that act as truths we embrace. They drive us because they provide a feeling of certainty about what something means, and its value. A belief is both mental and emotional. It is imbedded in the mind as well as the heart. Beliefs precede and determine actions and we fight for them with fervor. There is a correlation between beliefs and behavior. When we believe something, we act congruently with the belief. Logic isn't important in how we come to arrive at it. Since we don't know what reality is, we form beliefs to make sense of the world. They are very powerful because we put so much faith in them. When we cannot see anything outside of a belief it becomes self-limiting. This creates a box and we are only privy to the information contained within it. We are bound by the ignorance of anything outside of that box.

Beliefs direct our attention, which affects the quality of our lives. For example, Nancy may believe she's overweight, and find it to be unattractive. Her perceptions would then focus on her body fat and cause her misery. On the other hand, Gladys, who is also overweight believes it's sexy to be large and is happy to look that way! She believes that body types don't determine the qualities of attraction, or that larger bodies are actually more desirable. The same situation can be viewed entirely differently.

We act according to our beliefs, whether or not we are aware of it. Asking ourselves if they are shaping the life we want is critical. If not, why are we holding onto them? Beliefs are easily imprinted upon us throughout our youth. For some of us, limited beliefs are all we've known. Others have benefited from an environment that lays a foundation for positive beliefs. Our experiences are shaped from either of those two perspectives. Beliefs always attract situations, people and events that resonate with them.

Life in Crisis – Rainy days and Mondays get Leanne down

Event:

Leanne lives alone in a small apartment in Austin, TX. She's 23 years old and usually heads to the nearest coffee shop for some "get-up-and-go" every morning. Leanne believes that the song "Rainy Days and Mondays" was written for her. She believes it so much in fact, that she is always depressed when Sunday nights roll around. Her mood begins to shift as she considers what Monday will look like. When her alarm clock goes off Monday at 7:00 a.m., she is in full depressed status before she even gets out of bed. Her Facebook post says it all... "Another Monday... Just shoot me." As she wanders into Whole Foods to report for her duty as head chef in Prepared Foods, she pours her dark mood over the entire team. It spills over into the rice and beans she's preparing and now, even the food carries her darkness. That mood lasts until she clocks out. As the week goes on, things are starting to look up for Leanne. It's Thursday morning and she's starting to get excited. But Leanne didn't account for the change in weather and it's going to be a soaker. Clouds are moving in quickly. Realizing this, Leanne starts to get out of bed and immediately turns on depressing music because it's a rainy day and she's committed to being miserable. Unfortunately, that means another day of darkness for the rice and beans. And Whole Foods wonders why their Prepared Foods sales have dropped. Don't look at me, thank Leanne!

Synopsis:

Leanne's distorted beliefs have conditioned her reality so that when it's Monday or raining, she WILL BE miserable. She's created the rules she lives by and is committed to them. Her misery is a function of her distorted beliefs and perceptions. She has no idea of how to be happy on Mondays because in her mind, she's not supposed to be that way. She is committed to one way of looking at Mondays and rainy days. Although she feels helpless and doesn't know how to change, all she knows how to do is respond the way she's always responded. Well Leanne, how's that working for you, dear?

Away from Pain

When life isn't working, we are motivated to move from an undesired to a desired state. To accomplish this effectively, we must know clearly what it is we want. This means articulating a clear desired outcome.

If we're living in pain and want to have a different emotional experience, we're going to need a series of new beliefs, which will essentially create a new identity. The best option available to counteract pain and suffering is to understand the value of inner peace. As we value peace, we seek opportunities to have that experience. A belief that it will make us happier, drives us to assume the identity of a peaceful person. We must envision what a peaceful individual would look like, decide to become that person, and then take on the appropriate beliefs.

We become incentivized by beliefs that this new identity will deliver more friends, the ability to handle difficult situations, and overall happiness. With so many apparent benefits, we are now inspired to pay close attention to our lives. Therefore, as we value peace we are inspired to move toward it.

You may be a confrontational and angry person. If you want to be a cooperative person, what beliefs would you need to have? To want to be cooperative, you'd have to believe that being that person will make you happier. You'd probably believe that it's more fulfilling to be cooperative rather than disagreeable. You might believe that you'll be rewarded with promotions or increased salary.

Then, you'd naturally start noticing how cooperation delivers positive results and start realizing what being confrontational is costing you. Increasing your awareness of the benefits such as friendships, relationships and good feelings would shift your perceptions and beliefs, and therefore, your reality.

Life in Crisis – The blame game

Event:
Cassy is a 40-year-old accountant living in Denver who enjoys skiing, yoga and driving through the mountains. She is precise and makes everything about order, rules and discipline. She has everything calculated to the nth degree, including her schedule. On a crisp fall afternoon, Cassy set out for Aspen to enjoy the foliage and meet a friend for lunch. She was running late when she stopped at the Twin Pines shopping center for a quick Jamba Juice. Edward is 65 and a retired school teacher who lives on the outskirts of Denver. He was going to see his mother, who is very sick and in a nursing home community. He stopped at the same Twin Pines shopping center to pick up some flowers for her. Leaving the center, they backed their cars out at the same time, causing a collision. It was unclear who, if anyone, was at fault. Cassy became irate and threw open her car door to confront Edward. She was fuming. As Edward slowly rolled down his window, Cassy had already launched into a tirade about his negligence. She called him an old man who didn't deserve to be on the roads. Threatening him with a call to the police, she ordered him to speak with her insurance company and admit fault. To Cassy, there is no way she could be wrong. It had to be Edward's fault. It's the end of the discussion, as if there ever was one!

Synopsis:
Cassy is often wrong, but seldom in doubt. She simply cannot imagine herself to be at fault or to have any faults. She can't

afford to be wrong, because she's always played by the rules and never gotten in trouble. She cannot imagine being responsible for anything that doesn't turn up roses. Using Edward as a scapegoat lets her off the hook for her imperfections. In this manner, she refuses to look at herself, and what being in a rush might have caused her. Blaming someone else is an opportunity to avoid looking at ourselves, and the role we might have played in the experience.

Reflections:
Cassy's identity is tied up in being right. The blame game stems from a belief that always starts with a "me versus you" scenario. We can't see ourselves as being "right," unless someone else is "wrong." This approach strips away compassion and forces us into perceptions that serve only us. We can't be selfless under these conditions. It's a zero-sum game, where we win when someone else loses. The sad thing is that there is no positive resolution when it comes to blame. Believing that we are always right and someone else is wrong is a distorted perception of life. It reinforces the myths of invincibility and a blameless nature. Unchecked, this person could easily become a sociopath. We can also blame ourselves for everything, which is equally damaging and unhealthy.

The Costs of Limiting Beliefs

Since identity is the result of beliefs, which are a result of perceptions, which are driven by values, Tom's case illustrates how limiting beliefs disempower. Assume that Tom needs an orderly and clean environment to think clearly and work productively. From this, we can assume that Tom values cleanliness, order, symmetry and production. In terms of perception, he will be looking at the order or disorder of any environment.

This manifests as Tom's belief that when an environment is clean, his work and focus will be better. He believes that a lot of people around creates a messy experience. For Tom, order is a sign of an organized mind. He thinks that messy people have messy brains. He also believes that people who don't make their beds, are lazy. Tom believes that productivity is very important, and that ritual is like Heaven.

There's nothing inherently wrong with Tom. What's potentially negative in all of this is when he is exposed to a disorderly, noisy, crowded, smelly, or uncomfortable environment. Since he doesn't control 100% of the environments in which he operates, Tom is highly subject to a negative experience just around any corner. This affects his need to control the environment. Judgment is a natural by-product of his need for order because it's difficult for him to accept anything that doesn't match his values. Tom will make messy environments mean that others are a bunch of children who haven't grown up. It becomes a limiting belief because he has built a box around the world as he wishes it to be. When the world doesn't look that way, he doesn't function well. It also negatively affects his relationships. Tom will have trouble relating to others who don't follow the same discipline, causing him to undervalue them.

Tom suffers from false self-esteem because he experiences it from outside stimuli. A powerful self-esteem would say – "I feel OK wherever I am because I'm grounded, regardless of the environment."

The source of our frustrations stems from limiting beliefs and distorted perceptions. Values affect perceptions, perceptions affect beliefs and beliefs affect our identity. If we wish to see the world differently, we must deconstruct each component and reinvent ourselves as we desire.

KEY PAIN POINTS OF PEOPLE WITH LIMITING BELIEFS AND PERCEPTIONS

- Limiting beliefs generate unhappy results.
- Our beliefs, perceptions and values are tied together. One affects the other.
- Events are not inherently good or bad, but our perceptions and beliefs make them so.
- Our attachments to limiting beliefs keep us stuck in negative emotional states.
- Beliefs create reality. Therefore, a limiting belief will deliver an unhappy reality.
- Evidence reinforces our beliefs. We are evidence seekers. Perceptions are tuned in to what we already think and believe.

Language of Distorted Beliefs and Perceptions

"I can find something wrong with anything."

"Things will get worse before they get better."

"I can't enjoy today because misery is coming tomorrow."

PART III

THE POWER OF LOVE

"When you know yourself you are empowered. When you accept yourself you are invincible." - Tina Lifford

CHAPTER 11

STURDY, STABLE LOVE

"I will not adjust myself to the world, I am adjusted to myself."
- A Nin

Love Defined

Clearly, there are many ways to act from a position of fear and those actions don't lead to peace. Fortunately, there is another option. The opposite of fear is love. Acting from this frame of reference sets the stage for an empowered, happy and peaceful life. Love has been expressed and defined in different ways. For this book, we're defining love as the willingness to work on ourselves so that we can show up fully in the world. When we love ourselves, we're in the best position to love others well.

We can also view love as a filter. We know events are always happening and we have the choice to view them from this perspective, rather than a fearful one. This allows us to see things through a positive lens and create the experience of being OK and empowered with anything that happens.

Self-reliance means leaning on our emotional faculties to get through life's turbulence. When we don't demand anything from anyone, our relationships are purer. They no longer come with intent to satisfy a longing or a need to feel complete. When we love ourselves, we're more apt to give others a "get out of jail free" card in terms of being responsible for our emotional well-being.

The Impact of Our History

How we were raised directly affects whether we experience events through love or fear. Many of us come from homes that were based in a spirit of fear, scarcity, and lack. For those of us with that background, it is our responsibility to make peace with it. Although we might like to shift the blame to someone else, blaming others for the past will do no good in the present.

Our past influences our perspective and definition of love. What we've been told about it and how we've experienced it will affect our world views. If we've lived in a dysfunctional family, our approach could be tainted and ineffective unless we change. A dysfunctional parent exhibits different expressions of love than a functional one. Thus, our understanding of love is commonly affected by our history. Although we can't erase a negative past, we can move toward a healthier version of ourselves in the present.

Love of Self

As well as we love ourselves, is the extent to which we can love others. This means it's completely relevant and important to engage on a journey of self-love, which means honoring our personal truths. We must acknowledge and communicate how we feel to love authentically. Living in this manner, we can more readily connect with our power. A good way to do this is to look at ourselves and ask, "what are my needs and are they being met?" Self-inquiry is not intended to make oneself wrong, but to generate greater awareness and self-reliance.

Understanding that we alone are responsible for our personal happiness and well-being is tantamount to our development. Other people can affect us positively or negatively, but ultimately the responsibility is ours for how we respond. What's important is that we hold ourselves accountable for what we're feeling and not someone else. Moving toward self-love, it's helpful to articulate clear boundaries to clarify our positions.

Love for Others

Doing the work on ourselves is an act of love, especially when the motivation is to improve our relationships. By working on ourselves, we eliminate the demand that anyone else must carry our baggage and be responsible for our happiness. We then free them up for their own inner journeys and engage authentically without an agenda. We can create an experience for others that is so abundant, they freely choose to enter our world. Our compassion allows us to nurture and lift them up by celebrating their choices.

Love packs an emotional wallop when its presence is known. It has the power of both intensification and transformation. To experience the deepest sense of connection, purpose, and relationship, we must tap into its power. Being able to take a stand for another is the result of our self-love. It has the potential to bring out our best and lay the foundation for spreading love.

Loving Powerfully, Living Powerfully

Living from love is about simply abiding in the fullness of self-expression. There is no concern of reward except for the joy of life's journey. There is no feeling of hardship and we act without demands or expectations.

Dependency on others always finds a way to use the person we're leaning on, to create a false sense of security. When we're self-reliant, those around us feel better about themselves because we're not using them to make ourselves feel complete.

Emotional insecurity always leads to fear because there is a sense that something is missing and can only be filled by something outside of ourselves. Fear will cause us to use others for personal gains. The more insecure and dependent we are on them, the stronger the ties that bind. When self-reliant, all things become possible. We can let go of old patterns or thoughts that no longer serve us. We can choose to accept the realities of life, even conditions with which we are not in agreement. Living in abundance, we know that we are enough and can handle anything. With positive beliefs and thoughts, we operate from a position that everything is OK. In this way, love is liberating.

Benefits of Emotional Mastery

It's easier to interact with people exhibiting a high degree of emotional mastery. When we're self-reliant, we're not in a holding pattern waiting on someone else to confirm our sense of self. We comfortably take initiative and are responsible for every outcome. We don't blame, don't make excuses, own our actions, and accept the results without drama or negative meaning-making. The act of loving, itself, is sufficient reward. What transpires is much less important than our commitment to loving. We are fully present to the experience, because we don't have negative self-talk operating in the back of our heads. Our informed actions afford us the experience of a peaceful nature and a stronger sense of self.

Others feel peaceful around us as we project that calming essence. This creates an environment of relaxation and reflects our inner stability. As we love, we are essentially spreading it to everyone with whom we connect. This serves as an example for others as to what's possible and encourages emulation. All relationships benefit from individuals who are willing to master themselves.

The Opposite of Love

Failing to act with love means that we have defaulted to fear. We can recall from the first half of the book, the upset those actions ultimately create. When we fail to act with emotional maturity, we will always look to someone else or outside circumstances to make us feel happy, complete, or relevant. The disadvantage to others is that we pull them into whatever we create, even if it's chaotic. We are certain to engender a spirit of misery with everyone. We use others by leaning on them to fill our voids. This sets the foundation for pathological relationships. Pain and disappointment can often be attributed to possessiveness and attachment. Distress results from dependence and creates feelings of emptiness. Desire can produce a hunger, driven by a sense of scarcity. The cup may appear to be so big that it can never be filled. When we hunger for something, it controls our behavior and the price we pay is high.

Impacting Others

We attract at our own level of wellness. The behaviors we exhibit are reflected to us by others. Spreading love, we can begin to experience the interconnectedness between our actions and other people's actions. We see how one action affects another, creating ripple effects that powerfully impact and ignite relationships. Fear is disconnecting, while love is connecting. When we are not fearful, we are capable of acknowledging, accepting, and honoring everything around us.

Love gives us a spirit of compassion and the capacity to celebrate others. When we feel positively about our experience in life, we are motivated to share that positivity with others. When we act from fear, it is exhausting. When we act from love, we can stop identifying as a victim and reinvent ourselves as creators. Energized and rejuvenated, this allows others to see what maturity looks like for emulation.

Love in Motion

Love is about consideration for others while at the same time taking care of ourselves. Unlike enabling, it involves letting our positions be known while at the same time, respecting theirs. While love is supporting others, it is not about sacrificing our needs to satisfy someone else's. It is OK to sacrifice our wants if we choose! Examples of a need is: "I need my alone time. I need rest. I need to eat." Examples of a want is: "I want ice cream tonight. I want to watch a television show. I want to go to a movie."

Practicing love, we allow others to be where they are at their level of personal development. At same time, we allow them to experience the consequences of their actions and attitudes. It's a loving act to help others get their pictures big enough to see what they need to do to grow and develop!

Life in Crisis – It's a dog's life

Event:
Andrew lives in Jacksonville, where he moved 3 years ago. He is a successful IT professional, 30 years old and lives with 2 other roommates. They all have known each other since they

were 12 years old, growing up in Nashville. Their relationships are great. They enjoy spending time together, going on group dates and supporting one another through the issues of life. Andrew's sister, Amelia recently quit her job in Nashville and was considering moving to Jacksonville. She wanted to move in with Andrew and his roommates, whom she also knew growing up. They were all in agreement that it would be a great addition to the team and were supportive. Everyone was making plans for the big move, a few months away. Andrew decided to visit Nashville in the meantime and drove up to see his family and make more definitive plans with Amelia.

The trip home was going great when Andrew stopped in to pay a visit to Amelia. Upon entering her home, he noticed she had recently adopted a dog from the animal shelter, named Corky. Andrew was taken aback by Corky's aggressive nature, noting how he frequently lunged at him and growled over the entire weekend. Amelia mentioned that she intended to bring Corky with her to Jacksonville. The drive home consumed Andrew with doubt. He had two small cats and was concerned for their safety as well as the safety of the roommates with an aggressive dog. So, he wrote a very polite email to Amelia explaining his position to her. She took offense to it and told him to "forget it" and that she would live alone in Jacksonville.

Andrew followed up that email with 2 more, imploring her to forgive him for his explanation and that he was sure they could work out a solution. He didn't hear back from her and was so worried that he'd ruined a relationship with Amelia over Corky. His roommates were more concerned that he didn't feel OK articulating his position. They told him he seems to always need to have everybody get along at the expense of his peace of mind. Amelia didn't return his calls and he sunk deeper into remorse.

114

Synopsis:
Andrew confuses love with compliance. The need for everyone to get along trumps his needs. No wonder he lives in chronic anxiety, trying to make peace with everyone. Although he can't see it, everyone else can. Loving someone doesn't mean you have to agree with everything they say, do or think. But loving yourself does mean honoring your position and speaking your thoughts. Andrew must learn that it's ok to love someone and still have a different position. When he feels the freedom to speak his truth, his ability to love himself will make him a better brother and friend to everyone else. As for Amelia, she might consider allowing someone to have a different position and not make it a cause to get defensive or angry. There's a lot of growth possible here if each party is willing. Will they make it, or is Andrew in the dog-house?

Love is acknowledging another person's position, which is not the same thing as agreeing with them. Acknowledging means to help them feel heard and understood, which establishes a bond of understanding. Sometimes our positions don't bring us happiness. Part of love is considering each person's stance, understanding that there may not be an amicable agreement in the end. While expressing our positions, it's important to let others know how we feel. We don't want to make anyone else wrong by invalidating them, but it is emotionally mature to communicate how we feel about the issue at hand.

Love can be like medicine because of its transformative effects. It can help move someone out of depression, illness and destitution. Love is a connector and we all need it for survival. It is also an attractor because we energetically bring to ourselves what we radiate.

Love's Effect on Our Still Point

Each morning, we can awaken with excitement and anticipation. Anxiety can be replaced with enthusiasm and apprehension can be replaced with anticipation. We can enter the day believing that no matter what happens, something good will come of it. We can choose to look for the good in every event, rather than focusing on the negative. When we encounter others, we may consider ways to assist them on their journey, rather than wonder how they can make our lives more comfortable. We can acknowledge with compassion, the hurt others might be going through. This can lead to a more supportive, generous and giving dynamic. Love is a super-highway to reaching our Still Point and when applied daily, it creates a positive reality and delivers peace of mind.

CHAPTER 12

LIBERATION BY LETTING GO

"Letting go doesn't mean that you don't care about someone anymore. It's just realizing that the only person you really have control over is yourself." - Deborah Reber

The Nature of Letting Go

There is an art to releasing our attachments to things we desire, and it involves letting go of distorted thinking, judgments, demands, expectations, control or attachments. Letting go is characterized by an attitude of essentially being able to go with the flow. In that moment, we can accept the truth that we're not in control, and never were anyway. The qualities occur from a position of strength, not weakness. Ultimately, we're all subjected to outside circumstances and must work to become more adaptable.

Consider the person madly in love, whose partner breaks off the engagement. They are faced with the choice to either continue holding on, clinging with desperation, or allow life to move forward. Letting go is grounded in a belief that everything will be alright, regardless of the outcome. Without it, the prospect for inner peace will be diminished. If we don't feel safe in our own soul or feel like we can't handle what might come from another person's actions, we may resist going with the flow. On the other hand, when we feel secure, we won't feel the need to cling for dear life.

Perhaps you know a woman who has held onto a grudge for years. Let's assume she had an abusive mother, who ignored her throughout her childhood. Holding on to the anger leveled against her mother will do her no good. In fact, it acts as a barrier, preventing her from experiencing inner peace. Releasing the anger toward her mom would free up internal space for joy.

The Effects of Letting Go

Relinquishing resentment is paramount to our happiness. Trusting that the universe (God) is in charge and that our well-being is cared for, makes it easier for us to surrender. Finally, surrender is an action. Consider the young gay man in Small Town, Iowa, who has been seeking society's approval. He hasn't gotten it from his pastor, his church, his parents, or his peers. This is a critical moment of personal development when he must decide if he wants to continue caring about the approval of others. Will he let go of the need for someone to tell him he's OK, or succumb to the thoughts and feelings of a disconnected community?

This happens daily across the globe, and our responsibility is often to simply relinquish the need for approval. To release it, we must believe in our own power; especially when we know nobody may be coming to our aid. We may never hear words that affirm us. Under those conditions, it's vitally important that we move on with courage. In every circumstance, moving on is a willed experience. In that moment we say, "My well-being is more important than someone else's opinion."

Letting Go is not Denial

There is a distinction between letting go and denial. One is a deliberate emotional release from bondage. The other is equivalent to dismissing the reality of what is in front of us. When we don't acknowledge what we feel, those feelings don't go away; they remain inside. The pain we stuff down always finds its way back in a more pronounced manner than when we first went into denial. This affects us unconsciously and delivers more misery. Whatever we deny, finds its way back. Therefore, it's critical to address the emotions that arise. With increased awareness, we can choose healthy actions that lead to inner peace.

It takes great strength to release ourselves from an attachment. Being in touch with our emotions sets the stage for making conscious choices. A high degree of emotional intelligence pushes us toward love-based actions over fear-based actions.

The Joys of Letting Go

There are so many benefits that we receive from the act of letting go. Let's start with amazing peace of mind. It is liberating to surrender the responsibility for how someone receives us, our words, or our actions. When we are not charged by what someone else has done or said, we can exhale and relax. When we are no longer clinging to a desired outcome or response we experience a sublime peace of mind because the pressure is off everyone. We open the door for what is meant to enter our lives and to new possibilities that we might never have considered. A positive foundation is built when we are living with trust and belief that everything is going to be alright.

Life doesn't end when we don't get what we want. Actually, that's the point where it can begin. We don't always know what's best for us. A lot of what we desire is driven from our sick, compulsive, and addictive nature. It's a lot like the adage, "be careful what you wish for, because you just might get it." Our desirous nature often delivers unpleasant outcomes. If we're not healthy we don't typically get healthy results. When we let go, we are releasing that grasping nature.

A taste of inner peace arrives when we allow others to authentically express themselves. As we begin to feel OK within ourselves, it becomes much easier to accept what we might have previously labeled as "unacceptable" in others.

Increased energy is a natural by-product of not being drained by someone's actions. Rigidly pursuing a specific outcome can also drain our energy. Letting go is the key to creating inner joy and vitality.

The Art of Letting Go

It's easier to let go when we believe that life is good. Further, acknowledging that whatever happens is meant to happen and that we have no control over the results, places us in a position to surrender. Accepting the worst-case scenario is an effective tool for releasing our need to control outcomes. By facing the struggle, we discover our emotional strength.

This requires exiting our comfort zones and stepping into the unknown with courage. The more we practice this, the more comfortable we become, inhabiting a space of possibility. Allowing others to be who they are and learning to manage our "should's," moves us closer to acceptance. Relinquishing the need to have it our way gives us perspective from a higher vantage point. The art of letting go is a balance between communicating our wants, desires, and needs but without attachment to their outcomes.

The 7 Obstacles to peace provide a perfect starting point to identify what needs to be released for our peace of mind. Each of these represent the primary filters that must be left behind to live a life of emotional mastery. Releasing the inclination to act from these vices means parting company with old patterns and knee-jerk reactions. Thus, as we let go of one thing, we must be prepared to move toward another. Replacing these negatives with love-inspired actions, such as acceptance, is necessary to neutralize a situation or event.

Forgiveness is the ultimate act of making peace with our past. Let's face it, the reality is that we have all been hurt or will experience hurt in our lives and are doing the best we can with what we have. Everyone has weaknesses and blind spots, and being imperfect, our actions might unintentionally cause pain. Realizing this, it's easier to forgive others, which is like setting a prisoner free and then realizing that prisoner is us!

Resentment harms the person who is holding onto the memory. It's important to forgive because it frees us from bitterness, anger, hatred and resentment. Four groups of people worth consideration would include our parents, former and current intimate relationships, all others who have caused us grief, and of course, ourselves.

Perhaps understanding the role we played in each of these hurtful relationships will cause us to dig into our own sense of self and assume responsibility. This sets the tone for relationships where blame is replaced with maturity. Each day we grow and become different people. That part of us that did something silly, senseless or cruel, is not the same "us" that is here today.

A 3-Step Method to Letting Go

This method for letting go relies upon finding good in the middle of an experience that allows us to trust the process and change our perceptions. For example, Elizabeth owns a town-home. It's the middle of July and her air-conditioning unit just broke. She now must get it fixed or replaced immediately.

Step 1 – Acknowledge your emotional response. Don't live in denial.

Elizabeth must acknowledge that she's bothered that her air conditioning unit is broken. Don't live in denial. It is what it is. It's hot, she's sweaty, and it's an expense she wasn't expecting. She's understandably annoyed.

Step 2 – Decide what you want to experience.

Elizabeth wants to feel differently. She doesn't want to feel the rage, anger, frustration or hopelessness that comes along with a broken air conditioner. Elizabeth decides that she wants to feel peace. She has chosen something different than her knee-jerk emotional reaction.

Step 3 – Acknowledge the inherent pain of not letting go and choose something different as an act of self-love.

By letting go of the requirement that the air conditioning unit never break down, she's more capable of going with the flow. The only thing Elizabeth is in control of, is her response to events unfolding. Her upset about the air conditioning unit breaking is an indication that she's operating with demands and expectations. Self-scrutiny would reveal that her upset is attributed to her attachment that the air conditioning unit work properly. Understanding that operating from the left side of the

Emotions Matrix (pg. 5) will always yield misery, makes it easier to make a different choice. The only other option is to operate from the right side, which is guaranteed to deliver peace of mind.

TOOL-KIT

• Letting go liberates us when we release our attachments and are no longer held in emotional bondage.

• Letting go creates space for something new to enter our lives.

• Surrender moves us away from something to which we may be strongly attached and is causing us pain.

• Forgiveness is a gift to ourselves that releases us from unnecessary suffering.

Language of Letting Go

"I release my grip and flow with life's current."

"Everything is happening exactly as it should."

CHAPTER 13

INHALE, EXHALE, ACCEPT

*"My happiness grows in direct proportion to my acceptance,
and in inverse proportion to my expectations."
- Michael J. Fox*

About Acceptance

Acceptance is managing our emotional responses to events in a way that allows us to cope with reality. We start by recognizing the difference between things we can change and those we can't. For example, I can't change the fact that there aren't enough parking spots in my apartment complex. I've accepted I'm going to have a difficult time finding parking when I return home from work and made peace with reality by realizing that "right now," this is the situation. If I'm secretly resentful, then I'm not living with acceptance because there is resistance to reality.

Attachments prevent us from being able to readily accept what's happening without emotional fallout. When our well-being is dependent on a specific outcome, we are attached and cannot possibly be in a state of acceptance. This makes it difficult to know peace because we are fighting against a reality that isn't delivering our desires. Our dissatisfaction does little more than intensify our frustration.

Acceptance involves prioritizing peace of mind over demanding circumstances to fit our liking. It doesn't mean we stop desiring something different; it just means that we aren't going to allow ourselves to be frustrated. We can pursue a different outcome, while choosing to not be annoyed by the current situation. Acceptance doesn't mean becoming lazy and rolling over in the face of adversity. It's realizing that some things in life can't be immediately changed and our happiness doesn't have to be put on hold until we get what we want.

Accepting Others

Accepting someone is a precondition to being a positive influence in their life. This means not making them wrong and allowing them to be the "mess" they may be. Acceptance is an act of unconditional love and is an excellent method for positively affecting change. Experiencing it generates a feeling of safety and enhances our receptivity to feedback and input.

A lack of empathy and concern for others means we can't allow them to just be. Compassion creates an environment fertile with acceptance. Opinions of others, lifestyle differences, things that happen to us, personality quirks and daily trivial matters, are all opportunities for us to generate empathy. Accepting others is the result of using our brains to navigate our hearts.

Part of this process is deleting the usage of "should." Should is a judgment and anything judgmental is non-acceptance. "Should" implies there is a proper way and that the current state-of-affairs is incorrect. Operating like this arrogantly presupposes a superior wisdom. Life is experienced through unique and individual viewpoints that negate the notion of a singular ideal. We're not always going to see eye-to-eye, so we must learn to acknowledge our differences to establish peace.

The Nature of Acceptance

Acceptance is an act of acknowledging that individuals are unique and have the right to their opinions. It doesn't mean that we're saying something is alright or that we're in agreement; it just means that we allow everyone to have their own positions without judgment.

Releasing our rigid positions paves the way for acceptance and delivers freedom. Surrendering releases us from preconceived ideas and allows us to flow with the current of life. We feel pain according to the intensity of our attachments. We don't have to like what transpires, but our pain can be reduced or eliminated by assuming responsibility for our actions. An accepting nature sets us up for a life of serenity because we have let go of attachments.

Self-Acceptance

It's important to accept ourselves if we desire to experience our Still Point. Rejecting who we are causes our self-esteem to suffer because we're unable to honor our true feelings. As a result, we make ourselves wrong and stop trusting our instincts. It's impossible to practice self-acceptance without practicing self-love. An overly critical nature communicates that we're not OK and will cause unnecessary stress. Self-acceptance affords us the opportunity to make mistakes without demanding perfection. There's no benefit to condemning our flaws and imperfections. In accepting all our qualities, it becomes easier to extend that grace to others.

We can't experience our true value until we stop criticizing ourselves. When we are accepting, encouraging, and forgiving, we allow more love to enter our lives. We struggle with self-acceptance when it's defined by being flawless. Just because we may not have the perfect body, doesn't mean we can't enjoy the one we have right now. Self-judgment implies an internal war is raging; a struggle between accepting where we are, versus where we would like to be. For example, it's OK to want a great body but not accepting ourselves until we have that body, will debilitate us.

Accepting Others, Accepting Life

Consider the notion that not accepting someone isn't going to change them. We frustrate ourselves by demanding they behave differently. These expectations arise from the inability to manage our own anxieties because we haven't fully accepted ourselves. To feel OK, we assert our standards on others and expect them to take on our way of thinking. This behavior discredits individuality and leaves others feeling rejected.

Attachment or resistance eventually leads to heartache, anxiety, and unhappiness. Taking steps toward acceptance makes life easier. It takes greater mental work and commitment but, in the end, the payoff is huge. We can see things as they are, without trying to make them what we want them to be. This allows us to move forward in life with strength, rather than constraint.

While resistance might appear to be borne from a personal crusade, the true warrior understands there is no battle, except with the self. Knowing a positive outcome results from an open mindset helps us to choose it. As we surrender, we align our insides to match the harmonious rhythmic pulse of life. Thinking there is a battle to be won outside of ourselves is what keeps us in non-acceptance.

We can desire something different without being triggered by whatever is happening. Acceptance is about allowing something to be there without needing it to change to be happy. It's about not allowing our peace of mind to be affected if something isn't the way we want it to be.

The Cost of Resisting

Resisting keeps us in fight mode and disrupts the entire pattern of our lives. This energetic frequency alienates those around us. People get tired of listening to our complaints. Resistance is characterized by grand-standing, complaining, being a victim, throwing a tantrum, and other fits of rage. Each of these actions reflects an individual's struggle, swimming against the current of life. Being in resistance is emotionally exhausting and physically depleting. We flail our arms against a wind that is not responsive to our wishes. There's a stubbornness of will or of the mind that characterizes non-acceptance. This often stems from a personal position that makes either someone or something wrong.

Although we may get to be "right" from non-acceptance, the costs are high. We often force our friends and family to deal with our convictions and pull them into a miserable cycle of mental distress. Now, it surrounds them whenever they're in our presence. They may begin to build resentment as they realize what it's costing them to be in relationship with us. Eventually our resistance may spell the end of many intimate relationships.

Not being able to accept creates a heavy emotional load because we're guaranteeing conflict. That heavy load weighs us down and ends up exhausting not only ourselves, but those nearest to us. Instead of resistance, we can acknowledge what is and suggest what might be possible. Proposing an alternative without the pain of attachment promotes a positive environment.

Tolerating

Some people think that tolerating is accepting. Actually, it is the act of putting up with something with which we're not in agreement. Resistance is still turned on, at a low flame, which could be amped up at any moment. Tolerating something means avoiding the issue but still being emotionally charged by it. Running away from confrontations causes inner conflict. This turmoil is the result of not being in integrity with ourselves. Because we have been withholding our true feelings, it begins to eat away at our peace of mind. What began as an effort to maintain peace is disempowering and does nothing more than create the illusion that all is well. Tolerating may be the first step in the right direction, but it retains a negative emotional wallop!

We must also be careful not to confuse tolerance with acceptance. For example, I might accept that a friend of mine has unresolved anger issues from childhood. I will not however, tolerate his fits of rage when they are directed towards me. I can accept where he's at in his personal development, but there are no laws that say I must enjoy being around him when he blows up.

Acceptance is not about enabling the individual and their unhealthy behavior. It's also not about making them wrong for how they act. In authentic relationships, both parties are free to state how the other person's actions make them feel. I'm able to tell him that it makes me uncomfortable when he's angry and what he does with that information is up to him. I accept that he's an individual with his own mind and can behave however he wishes. It's important to understand that just because I accept him, doesn't mean I want to be around his erratic behavior.

Why We don't Accept

It's likely we'll resist accepting conditions that make us feel uncomfortable. We usually desire to stay in our comfort zones and stick with the familiar. Whatever the circumstance, we are most often motivated to reject anything that doesn't align with our conventional ways of thinking.

When our ego stands to get hurt in the process, we often cling to our positions. When it is intertwined with attaining a specific outcome, the likelihood of releasing our attachment is minimized. As such, clinging to the ego's position is like an IV that gives us life. It can feel like death when we don't get our way.

Accepting does not mean we must do nothing. We can accept something and still disagree with it. Witness the politicians who lose elections but still stand for their beliefs. They must accept the results and deal with the loss, because denying the truth is delusional. To not accept is a rejection of the truth. Adapting to what is, allows us to prepare for the next step. We must see what is before we can facilitate what can be.

People often act from a position of resistance, tolerance, or denial. Many of the reasons for these actions may seem to make sense, but they all come with a cost.

The Benefits of Acceptance

Acceptance leads to a life of inner peace because it is an act of releasing our rigid positions. When our happiness is no longer contingent upon external circumstances, we have set up the necessary foundation for a life of joy. It liberates us and others from the illusions to which we're attached. We can handle life's ups and downs easier because we are less emotionally volatile. We embody an easy-going nature and enjoy the health benefits of a relaxed mind. We're much better company and others take notice and choose us.

When we care about ourselves, we make choices that ultimately enhance our lives. Do we care enough about ourselves and those around us to move toward acceptance? Moving this direction reflects a deep concern with our well-being and accomplishes the objective of inner peace.

Acceptance is the act of making peace with reality. How we accomplish this may vary. When we are allowing people and things to be what they are without an emotional trigger, we set the stage for acceptance. Recognizing the nature of the ego and eliminating it from the situation allows us to see things as they really are, rather than how we wish they were.

The path is not an easy one. Getting there means letting go of our fantasies, desires, and anything else that keeps us going in circles. This can be a painful process. However, this kind of pain is redemptive and more desirable than the neurotic suffering we experience when we're not accepting what is. Whatever we hold onto, whether it's a fantasy, wish, or dream, keeps us bound.

TOOL-KIT

• "Should" is a judgment. Anything judgmental is non-acceptance.

• Just because we are willing to accept a situation, doesn't mean we have to be satisfied with it.

• Acceptance is the act of making peace with reality.

• Practicing acceptance doesn't mean giving up on what we want. It simply means allowing ourselves to be content if things don't go the way we planned.

Language of Acceptance

"I'm OK with what is."

"It's not personal, it just is."

CHAPTER 14

COMMITMENT IS THE MAGIC WAND

"Unless commitment is made, there are only promises and hopes; but no plans." - Peter F. Drucker

The Path to Commitment

Commitment is the most efficient path toward creation. When we desire the most empowering results, it is incumbent upon us to move in that direction. This positions us perfectly to make a difference in the world. Helping others, personal growth, and finding a life partner are all things to which we can aspire. These can be accomplished when focused and intentional energy is applied.

When traveling, we typically follow the most efficient route to reach our destination. In our personal lives, we so often choose to follow the most inefficient paths. Why is it that in other aspects of our lives, we choose efficiency and effectiveness, but in our personal lives we avoid it? Commitment is like traveling on a super highway. While it will get us to a destination quicker and with more empowerment, there is nothing wrong with choosing to pursue alternate routes. Desires and preferences are like exploratory adventures. There is a time for each of these, and our responsibility is to understand the distinctions and make appropriate choices.

In exploring, we are choosing a more scenic route. It's off the beaten path and involves wandering around and basically responding to life. It can be exciting, exhilarating and colorful, but it doesn't lead anywhere in particular. We can draw conclusions, gain a better understanding of ourselves and have fun. Oftentimes, a period of exploration will lead to a commitment, but we must initially identify what it is we really want and value. Then our actions, laser-like in focus, propel us toward our goals. This will lead to stability, foundation and a strong sense of self because we know what we want. This is empowering and moves our lives in a specific direction. In this manner we are creators.

If something or someone is important enough, we will make the necessary effort. The areas of our life that take up the most time and energy are the areas to which we're truly committed. Our actions reveal them just as much as our commitments generate our actions. It's easy to see what we value; just look at what we do. If we say we want to become rich, but spend all day playing video games on the sofa, we're deluding ourselves.

Unlike preferences or desires, commitments require focus, intention, and action. The importance of any action we take is reflected by the effort expended. If we desire to have a significant other and we aren't doing anything about it, then it must not really be that important.

If we aren't producing the results we want, we must pay attention to our level of commitment. Is it really a priority or more like a preference or desire? Preferring things to be another way isn't enough to create what we want. When we are committed to having a new experience, we will have a new outcome. Our circumstances change when we have a clear determination.

Preferences and Desires

With preferences, we allow for a great deal of flexibility. These are experiences that we like or enjoy. We might prefer an apple to an orange, or Indian food to Mexican food. Regardless of the specific preference, they each have the same relatively low emotional investment. They may elicit a certain pleasure, but the pleasure isn't an overwhelming one that's life-changing. There is an Indian food place in Dallas that serves the best chicken tikka masala, but it's not like I would be depressed if I couldn't have it. It's just something I enjoy.

Preferences are spontaneous, and we will typically have many of them. We might prefer classical music to rock and roll. We might prefer blue to red and so on and so forth. Ultimately in the realm of preferences, we take them relatively lightly, and don't attach a great deal of meaning or emotional investment to them. They are often conditional, depending upon our mood or temperament.

As we move toward desire, the focus becomes more intense. In this realm, there is an appetite present. If we desire Mi Cocina Mexican food, we want to go directly there; do not pass go, do not collect 200 dollars. As such, there is an aspect of longing because we want to have something or someone specific. There is more passion and investment present. We might see another person who we feel attracted to and feel pulled to them. We're not interested in negotiating, whereas in preferences, we can change our position. In desire, there is a specific object that has captured our attention or imagination and we must have it!

We may have multiple desires, but far fewer than preferences, since they require more deliberate energy. In almost every situation involving a desire, there are deliberate choices made. We select that one thing, person or restaurant out of multiple options, and direct our focus. We are active participants in that process, whereas preferences can be activated from an unconscious state of mind. Desires are conscious because we move toward what we want.

The Nature of Commitment

Commitments are catalyzing agents that build momentum and makes things happen. The choices we make move us toward a desired future. Commitments are deliberate, made from a conscious state of mind, and we become highly invested in them. It's easy to see their empowering effect because in the experience of commitment, we become directors of our lives. From this vantage point, we can make anything happen because we are passionate about accomplishing our goals with conviction. Consider the couple who are in love. The passion that swirls between them is evident. Because of the high value they place on one another, their commitment is strong and enduring. Knowing that they are heading down a path with common objectives, cements the relationship and makes it real.

Our commitments imply a relatively rigid and inflexible position. Once established, we don't want to veer off in a different direction. If we must, there is typically an emotional price to pay. They provide a test to our integrity. Are we who we say we are? Do we do what we say we're going to do? The answers to these provide an indication of the degree to which we are committed. Every time we make a commitment, it tests the integrity of our word. A history of making and breaking commitments might imply a meaningless quality of words spoken and people might begin to doubt us. Each time we articulate one, our personal reputation is on the line. Doing what we say is a profound expression of our integrity.

There's an implied sense of responsibility, and commitments are usually not quick decisions. Typically, they involve heavy thought and consideration, requiring time and energy. With all these factors, we have far fewer commitments than desires or preferences. Sometimes our preferences and desires become commitments and provide a foundation for moving toward creation. This requires a more deliberate nature and maturity.

If we don't view something as a priority, we won't commit. There must also be something intrinsically compelling for us to exert the effort. Commitments carry with them a unique symbolism to the individual and must have a clearly distinguishable payoff. They must have the potential to generate personal happiness or be incredibly useful. We commit to things that have the potential for a positive outcome. Understanding the consequences of turning back from a commitment, we exercise great caution in making them. With limited time available, we must give up one thing to make room for something else.

Costs of Commitment

There are three primary costs to consider. There are things we must give up, things which we must invest and opportunity costs to consider. We must be willing to give up aspects of our freedom such as time and potential experiences to make room for something else. There is inevitably some type of investment required such as time, money, emotions and energy. When we choose one thing, we cannot choose another, and therefore realize an opportunity cost with each commitment. Aspects of our lives may be deleted to create space, and often the cost is letting go of something or someone we may really enjoy and love. Sometimes making commitments costs us an incredible amount of peace of mind and mental anguish. We must make them wisely.

Life in Crisis - The guy who said, "Marry me!"

Event:

Landon and Gloria were living together in a quaint suburb of Philadelphia. Gloria was building a life with Landon and embraced it completely. They had been dating two years when she started pushing for marriage. She was absolutely in love, but the affection wasn't returned by Landon with the same intensity. He worked long hours in retail and would come home tired and spent. His days could run 12 hours in length. Gloria worked shorter shifts with the same retailer. They met during a training session and it seemed like love at first sight; at least it was for Gloria. She would often hint at marriage. Finally, after enough talking, Landon half-heartedly asked Gloria to marry him. In truth, he wanted to stop the constant badgering. She went on Facebook and social media announcing their engagement while Landon was oddly silent. In fact, he never even "liked" her Facebook post. After 2 months of living the charade, Landon admitted he didn't want to be with Gloria as a partner. Broken glass, broken dishes, and broken hearts ensued. Gloria wondered, how did this happen?

Synopsis:

Landon was never really committed to the marriage. From the start, he felt pressured, coaxed, and coerced as a way of appeasing his partner. Landon had no emotional investment in getting married to Gloria. To him, it was just an empty promise, not even a desire or a preference. With such little investment, Landon had no problem cutting off the relationship. The repercussions of broken dishes and loud screaming were hardly enough deterrent for him to move to the next phase of his life.

Gloria, who was committed from the start, suffered the pain of disappointment and anguish. She wondered where she went wrong, but in truth, she only went wrong in the regard that she didn't see that Landon never really had a commitment to their engagement. Had she looked closely, she would've seen evidence everywhere.

Reflections:
Landon has some responsibility for misleading Gloria. It would have been more honest to address his lack of interest to her and let her find love elsewhere. Misleading others can be very damaging. It also means that Landon must have been getting something out of the relationship and didn't want it to end. He had issues of low self-esteem and being chosen by someone gave him a sense of acceptance. Unfortunately, it wasn't enough to move him toward commitment. That's still not an excuse for lying to Gloria.

How We Keep Commitments

Consider the dating couple. When both are equally committed, it's more effortless. When they're not, it's always more difficult on the person more heavily invested. In the case of Gloria and Landon, clearly there was a canyon of difference between their feelings for one another.

A degree of passion and personal intensity is necessary to keeping the flame alive. When it dies, so might the commitment. Some people may keep it simply because it's a matter of integrity. They may consider this to be more important than their happiness and peace of mind. In this case, continuing against their will becomes a by-product of that integrity and keeps them unsatisfied. In some marriages, the couple stays married even though the passion is gone. Finally, we keep commitments when the value is harmonious with the energy expended. Additionally, when the value exceeds the effort, it's easy to keep the commitment.

Avoiding pain or embracing pleasure can motivate us to alter our commitments. For example, Tom is in a passionless marriage and there is no intimacy with his wife. He is deeply troubled by this and on several occasions has been kicked out of the bedroom. Each passing day, Tom becomes more pained by the idea of a future without intimacy with his wife. Motivated by this pain, Tom is on the verge of seeking a divorce and finding a new relationship. Ultimately the decision to commit comes down to weighing the pleasure received, versus the pain involved. When pain exceeds pleasure, the commitment will typically erode. When pleasure exceeds pain, it will usually endure.

Life in Crisis - Yes means maybe

Event:
Andy was an agreeable guy, living in Iowa City. He didn't like confrontation and liked to see people happy. He was always excited to entertain a possibility, living footloose and carefree. He was a 30-year-old guy who was content and super satisfied with his life. Still, every now and then he would dream of a different world and talk about how he didn't want to "work for the man" anymore and was ready to spring out on his own. Trevor was a get-it-done guy. He was 42 years old, had worked a disciplined life, and was able to commit to a project. Trevor met Andy and was excited about a real estate development project to pursue. They agreed to work together and initially, both contributed equally. After a few months, Andy's intensity began to wane. He mentioned other things had arisen, and Trevor tried to be understanding. It seemed that every time Trevor made allowances for Andy's actions, he encountered more excuses. First it was meeting someone he wanted to date.

Then it was the need for down time. Finally, Andy had identified another project he wanted to tackle. This left Trevor with the frustration of either completing the project alone or working on it when Andy decided to be "available." He was frustrated and disappointed.

Synopsis:
Andy always said he wanted to be free to choose anything. Trevor didn't understand that also included working on a project that could potentially change his life and ultimately deliver to Andy the freedom he so desired. The problem is that Andy can't put in the time to get what he really wants, because he's always saying yes to things that give him short term gratification. A life of saying YES to everything means Andy isn't able or willing to commit to any one thing. His "yes's" are actually more like "for now's." Or perhaps, to Andy, commitment looks like a part-time engagement. If Andy could see his life clearly, he'd see that a lifetime of non-commitment has led him precisely to this place, and he can expect more of the same until he understands what real commitment looks like. Maybe he isn't really into the project, or he is much happier "working for the man," than he admits. Earth to Andy!!!

Advantages of Making Commitments

With the high stakes of making commitments and the costs associated, why would we make them? When we make a commitment, it's like a proclamation that we get to decide what is going to happen in our lives. There is a personal, empowering feeling about making things happen that thrusts us into the driver's seat. At the point of committing, we are building, creating and generating momentum.

There is a great deal of camaraderie in partnerships, and commitments can bring together communities of like-minded people, moving toward the same goal. Ultimately, our lives expand and reflect the power of our intentions. As creators, we stand as pillars, setting an example of a possible future for those around us. Our commitments create tangible results. They give us a certain amount of control over an aspect of our lives. The only things we have control over, is the amount of energy we dedicate to something and how we handle our responses.

The Effects of Commitments on our Emotional Well-being

Our personal growth is another aspect worth consideration. This might mean we make a commitment to acceptance, which is the act of suspending our own wishes and desires to see things as they really are and not how we wish they would be. A commitment to letting go will move us toward releasing what does not serve us and allow what is positive to come into our lives. To commit to empowering beliefs is to carefully regard what we hold as truths. This means evaluating them to assess how we might benefit from choosing new positive paradigms. Committing to positive perceptions requires us to choose viewing events and thoughts in a positive manner. This means taking steps and doing the work on ourselves that will ultimately change our lives.

When we truly desire something, the attainment of that goal depends upon our ability to commit to it. When we finally prioritize our well-being, we will move toward wholeness. That wholeness leads to a clearer head and a more integrated heart. Now, we can operate with personal power, creation, and peace of mind.

TOOL-KIT

- Preferences and desires are the weaker cousins of commitment. There is less emotional investment required. We will have many more desires and preferences than commitments.
- Commitments set us up for the role of "creator" in our lives. It is the fastest way to manifest our goals.
- We all have internal scales relative to what is important. We will make decisions and commitments based on the value they provide.
- Commitments require a great deal of energy, foresight, and consideration due to the effort that will be expended. They must be taken seriously.
- The choice to move away or toward commitments is affected by three things. How will it affect our integrity? How is it affected by an analysis of value vs. effort? How is it assessed on the scale of pain vs. pleasure?

Language of Commitments

"What I'm committed to, expands."

"When I am committed, I am a creator."

CHAPTER 15

ILLUMINATING BELIEFS

"Replacing limiting beliefs with empowering beliefs will bring you closer to realizing your dreams."
- Gillian Skeer

What is Reality?

Our realities are directly affected by our beliefs and perceptions. These are the components of life's complexities, difficulties and joys. A negative script will always result in a negative reality. The chapters in the first section illustrate this point. Therefore, it makes sense that positive and empowering beliefs will result in positive realities. Let's consider effective methods to create empowering beliefs, change the scripts, and change our lives.

First off, let's not beat ourselves up about our beliefs. There's a darn good reason why we took them on in the first place. Families, religions, schools, cultures, and media deliver them to our mental doorstep. As children we aren't in the position to fight the authority representing those belief systems. We agree with them because other people are also on board. Further, not agreeing with them would get us in trouble. Simply because some work for others, doesn't mean they will work for everyone.

Over time, we are conditioned to see life through our world view filters. As we age, we see their cracks and flaws. Our pain and suffering become red light indicators that something needs to change. That's when we start to question our beliefs and discover that they may have never worked at all. Today, we can pick and choose the beliefs with which we are in alignment. This affords us the possibility of framing things differently. It's time we reinvent ourselves according to what works for us and what generates internal joy.

How Beliefs Work

Our beliefs dictate our behaviors. These behaviors follow patterns and routines that reveal what's important to us. For example, I had a friend who believed black cats are bad luck. When he saw a black cat cross in front of him, he'd go the opposite direction to avoid it. One night, while driving on a dirt road in the country, he was shocked when a black cat leaped in front of his car. Because of his belief, he turned his car around and drove 20 miles out of his way to get home.

If we want to find the underlying belief, just look at the pattern. A belief produces multiple patterns and perspectives. Consider my friend above and his beliefs. He won't visit people at their homes if they have a black cat. Also, he refuses to go into pet stores. Evidence reinforces our beliefs. One time, he got horrible food poisoning after a black cat passed in front of him and that was all he needed to confirm his belief. His life will become an experience of constantly seeking confirmation. Thus, we can see how patterns can result in risk avoidance and cause us to seek safe and predictable comfort zones.

Whichever belief we choose to support, manifests our reality. There is as much evidence to back the belief that the world is dangerous as there is that it's safe. The question then becomes, to which belief are we committed? If we desire to experience the world as being safe, we must direct our efforts toward finding evidence that we are secure, and the world is safe. The health of our well-being depends upon the option to which we subscribe.

We know beliefs aren't serving us when we're unhappy, sad, fearful, lonely, desperate or disempowered. When faced with one that doesn't serve us, it's important to ask, "Why am I supporting it?"

Breaking Patterns

Why do we continue to focus on finding evidence that doesn't enhance the quality of our lives? We will search for proof to confirm our beliefs, even if it makes us miserable. We often get caught up in patterns that are difficult to break and settle into our comfort zones despite the upset they cause. Today, we have the power to respond according to our choosing. When experiencing an unpleasant emotional state, we can refer to the 7-step method to resetting beliefs available at the end of this chapter.

Placing blame on someone else for what we are feeling does us no good. Sure, someone's actions can upset us, but we ultimately have jurisdiction over how intensely we react to outside information. We can't always control what happens to us, but we can always control how we react to it. All answers are available when we search within. It takes a close examination of our internal dialogue to uncover why we do the things we do and why we react the way we react. An important question to consider is, "What must I believe in order to feel this way?" When we choose to look at ourselves, we are assuming responsibility for the feelings we've experienced. When we blame others, we take on a victim mentality and make ourselves appear helpless. Only when we assume accountability for our lives, can we truly guarantee our peace of mind.

Revelations

Our belief systems are revealed through relationships. We don't always have eyes to see what they are, but if we look carefully, we'll find them. For example, I might get hurt if my partner forgot my birthday. I have the choice to blame her for however I see fit. After all, her negligence caused me hurt. Thinking as such, I make myself a victim. The interesting thing is that she's not responsible for what I'm feeling. She might choose to comfort me and apologize, but at the end of the day, I'm responsible for my emotional well-being.

My reaction doesn't come from the event itself, but from what I tell myself about it. If I believe she doesn't care about me, then I will feel pain. If I believe she's been busy lately and is forgetful, then my experience becomes less dramatic and more empathetic. She's accountable for her actions, just as much as I'm responsible for my emotions. I can't force someone to behave a certain way, as they can't force me to feel a certain way. If the event causes me to connect with pain, it's my responsibility to have a blameless conversation with my partner. If I'm simply providing feedback, there would be no inherent reason for her to become defensive, because I've not made her wrong. If she creates pain for herself, that's her choice. Each of us is responsible for our unique reaction to an event.

Sharing personal truths helps to form an understanding of how our belief systems are operating. When we do this, we minimize the potential for misunderstandings and misinterpretations because we establish clarity and focus. For example, I might be very unhappy if my girlfriend nags me all the time. I can share with her my truth, that when she nags, it makes me feel incompetent. Sharing this gives her a chance to understand what I'm experiencing and an opportunity to speak with me differently.

If I do not give her this opportunity, then I might develop the belief that my girlfriend is annoying and doesn't think I'm a capable human being. I may grow to resent her. If I do not tell her how I feel, I run the risk of developing unfavorable thoughts about her that may not even be true. I can find evidence to support that she's annoying because of the way she treats me. Now when we go out, I may not be as affectionate, or do nice things for her. If this continues long enough, she may develop beliefs about me that say I'm not romantic, or I'm cheap because I don't buy her flowers. When two people in a relationship aren't sharing their personal truths, it can create a vicious cycle, comprised of many assumptive beliefs. This can ruin potentially great relationships.

What We Believe about Ourselves

Important thoughts and ideas that we must investigate are the beliefs we have about ourselves. What we think about ourselves affects how we treat others and our world view. For example, if I see myself as an unlovable person, I will see the world as an unlovable place. If I see myself as being accepted, then I will see the world as an accepting place.

We can create beliefs out of thin air as easily as adopting them from our families of origin or our social interactions. If we have evidence to back them up, they will remain. An excellent exercise to create empowering beliefs is to write down the ones we desire and find evidence to support them. When there is strong and supporting evidence, the belief becomes more real and foundational. It's important to adopt beliefs that don't have a lot of counter-evidence. For instance, I would not want to articulate the belief that I'm the strongest man in the world because I will be surrounded by counter-evidence, as my height, age and weight suggest otherwise.

We must connect with the pain caused by old beliefs if we truly desire change. Some questions that help guide us there are:

- *What is my current belief costing me?*
- *How has it held me back and negatively affected my life?*
- *What beliefs do I have about myself, the experience, and the other person to feel this way?*
- *Who would I have to be to get what I want?*
- *What would I have to believe to get the results I want?*

After we find evidence, we can begin to see ourselves differently. This reinforces our new way of being.

The Impact of Familiarity

There is a relationship that we have with the same old story we tell ourselves. It's familiar and it's something we've grown comfortable believing. When we try to tell ourselves a new and empowering version, it's like entering unfamiliar territory. We're not comfortable with it yet, so we don't like telling it to ourselves, even though it's beneficial. Sometimes it's more comfortable to stick with a debilitating story we tell ourselves than to venture out and create a new one.

For example, Jaime tells herself that she can't easily trust people because she's been hurt too many times. She has been telling herself this for years. She has developed a deep relationship with this thought and believes it to be true. When Joe and Dave give Jaime a new and empowering way of looking at herself, she resists because the idea is so foreign to her. She isn't ready to hear it, because there is so much personal evidence in her life to prove otherwise. The thing about beliefs is that they are self-fulfilling. If Jaime started telling herself a different story, she would empower herself to establish a new way of being. When she commits to collecting evidence that there is so much good that comes from trusting others, she will be able to let go of her familiar tales that people can't be trusted. We have the opportunity at any time, to change the plot, the characters or the ending of our stories. Acting from that vantage point ignites our personal power.

The Power of Foundational Beliefs

Our beliefs are interlocked with one another and exist on a continuum. One affects the other, which affects another, like a domino effect. As such, it can be said that beliefs lead to other beliefs. For instance, If I believe that God is judgmental, then I might think that every action I take is subjected to a biblical standard. If I believe that God is loving, then I might think that I will be forgiven for any transgressions committed.

It's so important to finally get to the root belief, which lays the foundation for how we experience everything. All our actions emanate from that position, both positive and negative. The foundation can either be identified as fear-based (God is judgmental) or love-based (God is loving). Fear-based actions such as judgment, control, and attachments fundamentally stem from fear-based beliefs. We wouldn't be experiencing judgment if not coming from a place of fear. We wouldn't be experiencing joy if not coming from a place of love. Everything grows from the root. It is our responsibility to connect with loving beliefs if we intend to have a peaceful and joy-filled life.

We are like bounty hunters looking for that piece of evidence that will either reinforce our beliefs or destroy them. When we're told something repeatedly, and we see everyone else's reaction, it serves as validation. On the other hand, when we have beliefs that are constantly pushed back, challenged or rejected, they become much more difficult to maintain. Our personal truths are either empowering or disempowering. Empowering ones make us feel full, expansive, happy, and peaceful. Disempowering ones leave us feeling crippled, helpless, and victimized.

Our emotions indicate how beliefs affect us and inform us of what's not working. Our incentive to move toward a new belief is predicated upon our degree of pain, which is our wake-up call. Nothing changes until we acknowledge the messages delivered from our emotions. We're just going to keep doing the same and getting more of it until we decide it's time to change our thinking.

7 Steps to Reset Beliefs

Step 1 - Articulate your current belief.

When we acknowledge a current belief, it means that we are getting real about what we think and feel. For instance, Tom's belief "money doesn't grow on trees," might mean that it's hard to make money and that money has an incredible value. It's not wrong, it's not right, it's just a belief. But the belief carries with it, implications.

Step 2 - Take personal inventory of the belief.

How does it make you feel? What has it created for you? What has it cost you? Tom's belief makes him feel insecure. To Tom, there isn't enough money out there in his world to make him feel comfortable. He lives in lack. He lives in fear. And he lives in constant vigilance, looking for opportunities to make money. It shaped his paradigm of "hard work results in making money." This costs Tom freedom because he's in bondage to an idea of his need to perform and apply himself diligently. He won't allow himself to have fun because that would be a waste of time. And as Tom believes, "money doesn't grow on trees."

Step 3 - Explore how your current belief prevents you from experiencing satisfaction.

• Is it forcing you to control something?

• What attachments keep you bound to it?

• How might it cause you to judge?

• What demands, or expectations are the result of it?

• What negative meaning might you attach to it?

• What other beliefs do you have that are preventing you from replacing it?

For instance, Tom is attached to the idea that money = security. He makes "money doesn't grow on trees," mean that money doesn't come easily and that it requires hard work to acquire. Tom is trying to control his anxiety about money by committing himself to a rigorous work schedule that allows him no time to enjoy life. Tom's relationship to money controls the way he lives his life, or doesn't live his life, depending upon your perspective. The belief about working hard for money places a heavy demand on his time and energy. His other belief is that money is the ultimate measure of success, which causes him to judge those who make less than him. Any one or all of these represent Tom's obstacles toward moving away from an existing belief.

Step 4 - Visualize how would you like to live your life

Tom wants to live free from the concerns he has about money. He wants to go out on the town and enjoy himself once or twice a week. He'd like to be able to rest his head at night without worry about how many hours he must put in the next day. He'd like to be happy about the things he buys, and not feel remorse each time he spends money on himself. Tom wants to live without a budget for every item in his life. Living in abundance would be his dream. Everything he touches might turn to gold.

Step 5 - What beliefs would you need to create this dream life?

Tom wants to move towards the belief "Money comes easily, and I live in abundance." Acknowledging that his old belief about money was causing him pain, suffering, and anxiety, Tom recognizes that shifting his belief is imperative to experiencing serenity about money. This will activate inside of him, the potential for the Midas touch. His new belief won't guarantee that he'll get there but not having it will guarantee that he won't. Fundamentally, Tom must identify himself as a person to whom money comes easily, to move toward that belief. We must be able to see ourselves as a new person if we want to become it.

Step 6 - Commit to finding evidence to support your new belief.

Evidence reassures and comforts our minds and affirms that we're going in the right direction. Tom must be committed to finding evidence to support "money comes easily, and I live in abundance." He will now grow in awareness of the subtle positive changes taking place in his life. Once he starts to notice them, they will begin to multiply. Each time Tom sees that his life is changing, he moves closer to his new beliefs. When he directs his focus toward the positives, they will expand.

Tom's commitment to finding evidence means he'll find even more, which will further enhance his conviction that he's headed in the right direction. It might appear as an experience of Tom's friend, Anthony. He hasn't worked a full-time job in 20 years and seems to be doing just fine. Anthony doesn't worry, and money always shows up for him. Maybe there's something that Tom could do different, and by looking at how Anthony lives his life, he can emulate it. Tom is actively involved in finding evidence to the point where he studies people, places and things, searching for validation. Meet-up groups, books or other friends and acquaintances are all opportunities to uncover the evidence he seeks. The proof is everywhere once Tom opens his eyes.

Step 7 - Commit to live from your new belief.

It finally becomes incumbent upon Tom to commit to the new belief. Evidence provides half of the solution to move toward change, and the other half is commitment. Tom must ultimately choose to incorporate the new belief into his new way of being. He may have to program it into himself daily until it becomes part of his unconscious. He may be pulled by the energy from the old belief, but he can choose at any time to engage the new one. The more he practices this 7-step method, the more Tom can apply it to any of his beliefs.

TOOL-KIT

- We can transform our unhappy patterns by changing our beliefs.
- We must desire a different outcome to begin the process of change.
- We can't always control what happens to us, but we can always control how we react to it.
- Our reactions don't come from the events themselves, but from what we believe or the stories we tell ourselves.
- Our beliefs are as strong as the evidence we provide.
- We can change the plot, the characters or the ending of our stories. Acting from that vantage point ignites our personal power.

Language of Empowering Beliefs

"My reality is a reflection of what I believe."

SECTION IV

A POWERFUL WORLD VIEW

"I know nothing, with any certainty, but the sight of the stars makes me dream." - Vincent Van Gogh

CHAPTER 16

MAKING MOVES

"Two roads diverged in a wood and I – I took the one less traveled by, and that has made all the difference."
- Robert Frost

A Fork in the Road

There comes a time in each of our lives when we ultimately face forks in the road. At these intersections, we recognize that important choices must be made, which require actions that ultimately deliver pain or peace. Understanding that we all face a series of decisions, it becomes clear how the choices we make have created the lives we live. The forks are often inspired by daily events and present an opportunity to make moves in another direction.

Recognizing that we have the power to tailor our response to events, implies a high degree of emotional intelligence. Those taking actions that deliver a happier and more peaceful life reflect a high degree of self-mastery. Some of us are not aware that choices exist and remain in comfort zones, subjected to reacting from a default program. This is often characterized by upset, isolation or difficult relationships. Alternately, we can direct our actions toward a positive outcome of joy, harmony, good health, profound relationships or peace. The paths we take direct our future. Therefore, we must choose carefully and act from an informed consciousness. "Am I making this decision based on who I've been or am I making this decision based on who I choose to become?"

Who We've Been

In a sense, we're programmed from the day we're born. Our DNA, families of origin, the churches, schooling, and the things to which we've been exposed, create or influence our points of view and frames of reference. The lessons we learn about success and failure are ingrained in our minds and hearts from childhood experiences. We're less free to choose in our youth because we typically do as we're directed. Those who don't, are considered rebellious children and are often administered all kinds of meds to temper their individualistic thinking and their desire for freedom. We begin to understand, through a series of actions and reactions, what we can and cannot say or do. We very intelligently begin to navigate the landscape based on the impressions we get from others. In a sense, the "who we've been" isn't necessarily "who we really are," but it is a historical perspective that was placed on us through expectations and projections of others.

The degree to which this has happened, and it does not resonate with our true sense of self, is the degree to which we experience anxiety. When we've been told we're someone, but our sense is, we're someone else, we are left as a splintered self and may suffer from anxiety, frustration or both. We long for like-mindedness and to know that we're not alone.

We want to know similar individuals who share supporting beliefs as a community. The problem is, we so often don't know where to find these people and we think we are terminally unique. We are in bondage to someone else's version of our lives until we liberate ourselves.

Coping as a Survival Technique

When our sense of self is in disarray, we open the door for anxious thoughts and inner trembling. We experience a day as a nightmare, feeling like we don't fit in, or we're not a good person because we didn't do what was expected of us. Living from this headset is so difficult and damaging that we often resort to coping mechanisms just to make it through a day.

Coping is a kissing cousin to addictions and compulsions. It's a way of avoiding an uncomfortable existing inner feeling. It has many faces, such as food, alcohol, porn, sex, video games, sleeping or withdrawal. Any of these done in excess can lead to addictions and serve as indicators that we're coping with something. At the surface, these may look like solutions to our inner dialogue because they take us out of the here-and-now and put us in a fantasy or illusory world. In that world, we don't' have to face what it is that ails us. We can retreat into the safety and comfort of our chosen method of disappearing.

But that world is also dull. It has numbed our senses and we just get by, looking for the next opportunity to initiate our coping mechanism. This requires a system, and some people have elaborate systems that become rituals. Consider someone who can't comfortably fall asleep because of their anxiety. This person may go through a step-by-step process to calm down before bedtime. This is probably more common than any of us realize, but it's only a temporary fix that doesn't address the real problem. What we're trying to avoid can easily feel like life and death. To the person experiencing it, this may seem real because of its intensity, and we experience either a fight or flight mode.

To take flight would mean looking for a diversion or an escape. Running away from a feeling is an acknowledgment of its power over us. Further, running away temporarily buries the very feelings we're trying to escape. This only makes the beast appear bigger and harder to deal with, the second time around. But how can we fight the beast inside when we don't have the tools or know-how? And when is fighting the best way, compared to allowing or accepting?

Modern day fight or flight issues might seem like survival is at stake because our responses are like those programmed in our DNA to deal with life or death situations; such as encountering wild animals. Today, however, our fight or flight mechanisms are typically generated from situations that are not actually life threatening. For instance, sitting in traffic, going to the dentist, trying to make ends meet, or being called to see our boss may each trigger a response that is rooted in our DNA, but not appropriate in its intensity. While we may feel that these situations are life threatening, this predisposition causes anxiety and frustration. It causes us to become over-agitated, overaggressive, and excessive. In the midst of this intensity, we will more often stimulate coping responses since we can't respond directly to the situation. As such, survival becomes more of the norm today than fighting, and is pervasive throughout society.

Continual refusal to deal with life's issues means that we must be committed to coping mechanisms that will always take priority. How can we possibly prioritize anything else when the situation feels like life and death? Those of us involved with heavy coping are so busy running away from our anxieties that our relationships inevitably suffer.

Another problem with a life heavily invested in coping is that oftentimes to get the same effect, we must increase the dosage. It creates a miserable existence and we can easily become enslaved to the thing that we believed would deliver freedom. When we run away from our issues, they remain unresolved and we are choosing to escape our reality, instead of addressing our problems.

Coping is a way of trying to manage outside circumstances so that we don't have to deal with our inner turmoil. It manifests itself through control, demands, expectations, attachments and judgments. When this drives our behavior, we're guaranteed a life of chaos.

Why We Choose Coping

Coping mechanisms keep us in our comfort zones because it keeps us from having to confront our inner demons and the things we don't like about our lives. It allows us to avoid dealing directly with our issues and doesn't really solve them. Why wouldn't we want to address our issues? Maybe we don't want to see ourselves as imperfect or broken. Families of origin and how they deal with things mean that coping can also be a learned behavior.

We try to avoid facing the things about ourselves that we may not like because it's unattractive, and it may require a lot of work. We avoid pain and discomfort at all costs, even when it is to our detriment. Coping represents the quickest and easiest way out of an uncomfortable situation, but ultimately leaves us feeling unresolved. If we were more concerned with resolving our issues instead of ignoring them, we would be living a more powerful and responsible life. Even though we know we're not perfect, we seem to go great distances to try and appear that way!

Choosing Who We Want to Become

A quiet confidence is the result of living the life we're meant to live. There is a resounding calm that we experience as we live authentically. Every day can be an adventure and every moment is pregnant with the opportunity for discovery. From that space, our consciousness grows and our awareness increases. There is always an opportunity for growth. Living authentically acts as a safety net because outcomes don't matter as much as the notion that we are home to ourselves. Living this way, we can choose to reset life events as we see fit. We are capable of being in anyone's company because we are no longer looking for something outside of ourselves to manage our anxieties.

Taking care of ourselves is apparent by our flexibility and how we handle the unpredictable. We can be thrown different curve balls in life without losing our peace of mind. Life moves from black and white to living color because wonder is everywhere. Discovering beauty in nature or under the simplest of circumstances sets us up for a life rich in texture. Everything is exciting because every situation is an opportunity for personal discovery. In this state of mind, we no longer need assurances because we embody the spirit of assurance.

A belief that everything can be handled is exhibited by people who live powerfully. There is nothing to worry about. We don't have to figure everything out and freedom abounds. Trusting ourselves gives us real power over rules, mandates or regulations intended to control us. We're free to interact, expand awareness, and act from a conscious head-set. We are much better equipped to commit to either goals or relationships. With this trusting approach, we can create more easily, and this becomes second nature. No longer burdened by the 7 obstacles mentioned in the earlier chapters, we are prepared for a peaceful existence.

Sharing either what we have, what we know, or who we are, we move toward the path of love. The desire to share indicates our level of wellness. In this manner, we put ourselves in the position to reflect on the gifts and qualities that have been endowed to us. When we've moved away from coping, our world shifts and though growth is ever present, there is a grace about the way we handle issues, confrontation and resolution. We can dance with life, and our world becomes spontaneous and colorful.

TOOL-KIT

- Coping is a way of dealing with our issues in a manner that doesn't actually resolve them.
- Coping is a way of trying to manage outside circumstances so that we don't have to deal with our inner turmoil.
- Choosing who we want to become is an aspect of creation.
- Trusting ourselves grounds us and generates an inner calm.
- Living powerfully is the experience of sharing our unique gifts and qualities and acknowledging them in others.

Language of Living Powerfully

"I am who I say I am and I do what I say I do."

"I embrace the fullness of life."

CHAPTER 17

SWIMMING IN GRATITUDE

*"Gratitude makes sense of our past, brings peace for today,
and creates a vision for tomorrow."*
- Melody Beattie

Gratitude Defined

Gratitude is a highly spiritual emotion, acknowledging our gifts, relationships and experiences. Taking inventory allows us to identify the positive aspects of our lives and generate an attitude of thankfulness. This sets the stage for a powerful emotional expression. Gratitude corresponds directly to our level of happiness. If we can't appreciate what we have, we won't be able to appreciate a lasting happiness for the things yet to come. Further, as we immerse ourselves in that spirit, we can connect with the abundance surrounding us. When we acknowledge the aspects in our lives for which we are fortunate, we can feel satisfied.

Moving toward gratitude begins with paying attention to the simplest aspects. If we can feel appreciation for simple things, such as a beautiful sunset, or a freshly cooked meal, it lays the foundation for happiness. Connecting with our blessings delivers us an attitude that's positive, productive, and empowering. Throughout this process, we learn to express appreciation for what we have and for those in our lives. An important note about gratitude is that it is borne from a state of consciousness. It's a process of taking responsibility for our thoughts. Consider it like putting the car in park, taking a deep breath, and inhaling all the positives surrounding us.

Generating Gratitude

There are many ways to be grateful, and it starts with taking on a different perspective. We can begin by acknowledging the smallest things we might otherwise overlook. As we put a magnifying glass over things that appear unimportant, their significance can be more readily seen and experienced.

Less difficult would be to look at our own lives and acknowledge how incredible it is to have security, a roof over our heads, the gift of literacy and the air we breathe. An appreciative outlook and increased awareness creates endless possibilities for gratefulness. Finding the good in every situation is a mindset, and one to which we can commit.

Being grateful for one thing can trickle down to being thankful for many others. For instance, being thankful for a job, taken to the ultimate degree, means I can appreciate that it pays for the life that I enjoy, my automobile and for so many other things that bring pleasure. When we talk about the spirit of gratefulness, there is a quality of bathing in its good feelings. Sitting in meditation, we can invite warmth and immerse ourselves in the moment. Since how we respond to our emotions delivers either misery or peace, it's important to identify how connecting with gratitude leads to happiness.

How We Experience Gratitude

Gratitude is a powerful force that affects all areas of our lives and development because it allows us to celebrate the things that we like about ourselves. In this way, it can help raise our self-esteem. When we count our blessings, it delivers a sense that our situations aren't as bad as we might have thought, and that we are valuable.

There is a seed of beauty carried within every circumstance, waiting to be revealed. Although we may go through terrible and difficult situations, even these have the potential for revelation and personal growth. It is incumbent upon us to locate those seeds, connect with them and appreciate the lessons learned.

For what things might we be grateful? We can be grateful for those qualities of self such as health, mind and experiences. We can appreciate others who show us the way and help us see ourselves more clearly. Gratefulness activates our personal power and releases us from fear. There is no room to be afraid when we abide in that state.

Being grateful helps us to see what we have and generates a feeling of security because we feel like we have enough. When we feel like we're in poverty, fear can take over our lives because it tricks us into believing that we're not OK. Living in abundance creates a sense of security because we know there will always be enough. This dispels our fears and leads to emotional self-reliance.

When we live in gratitude, we can find it easier to let go because we have so much. We can handle inconveniences when we recognize that the vastness of what we have dwarfs the slight discomfort of what we don't.

Gratitude and Wellness

Gratitude is a stepping stone to wellness that imbues a flexible mindset. This means we can go with the flow and appreciate whatever is happening in each moment. Freeing us up from old ways of thinking and attachments, gratitude paves a highway that moves us quickly toward our goal of peace and happiness. This quality of appreciation generates internal wellness where we don't have to control or act out scenarios to satisfy our selfish desires.

Gratitude sets the stage for our interactions with others. Another example of how it can move us toward wellness is to look at our attachments. They reflect a mentality of lack, compared to gratitude, which arises from a position of abundance. Why would we be attached to one negative thing when we know that we have a world of positive things happening to us?

Creating a Healthy Mindset

Generosity is expressed when we engender a spirit of gratitude. We share our resources, talents, or insights with others when we feel like we have enough. The act of giving builds community and enhances relationships. When we do something nice for someone else's benefit, it can form a lasting connection and impression. Future interactions carry with them a memory of the act of kindness.

Most of us have been recipients of another person's sharing. It could be friends, parents, or ideas. Kindness and generosity help to sustain a joyful life. Giving and sharing is an important act of love, which can multiply and eventually touch many people's lives. Gratitude reflects the spirit of abundance and giving is the physical manifestation of that quality. We have an innate desire to share and when we do, we connect ourselves to humanity. Those who receive these gifts benefit from enhanced self-esteem because giving sends the message that the recipient is valued. Like gratitude, giving is a conscious act where we become empowered from the choices we make to give.

Let's consider what the world would look like if giving suddenly stopped. It would be stagnant, sterile and disconnected. Withholding keeps the cycle of lack, territorialism, small-mindedness and fear alive. Sharing is the engine that keeps life in perpetual forward motion. When we give, we jump-start the engine. Our ability to relate compassionately to others activates an instinct to care. What could be more important than sharing our gifts?

Connecting Dots

We might click into gratitude for the car we drive. We then realize that having a car allows us to drive to a job. This job allows us to pay for a gym membership and at the gym we met the person who became our significant other. In this manner, we can begin to see that having a car touched many aspects of our lives and we can be thankful for each step of the journey. Taking these lines as far out as they can go, we can begin to see how one thing can affect many others. Not only can we begin to see the inner connection, we can also begin to feel it.

Living from the heart, we begin to sense specialness everywhere, and this gives us an extra sensory filter. It's like we're able to see and connect dots of which others aren't aware. As the connectivity grows, our reality expands. This enlarges both the size and scope of our personal universe, which generates a solid inner foundation.

Gratitude is an act of high emotional well-being. This conscious awareness elevates us higher and motivates us to live as a positive example to others. In this way, we can inspire people whom we might never know personally.

When we are swept in the energy of gratitude and feel its expanse, emotional triggers become less debilitating. It is an exceptional and effective action to take when we are feeling down and out. The results will most often leave us feeling grounded and secure. With a Universe that's "for" us, how can a simple uncomfortable event limit us?

Finally, gratitude is the ultimate antidote to entitlement. Society today reflects a degree of narcissism run amok. It's all about "Me" and what "I deserve." It changes the "I deserve" conversation to "I appreciate." There is so little joy to be had from a life characterized by entitlement and privilege. A life of deep appreciation positions us for joy around every corner.

TOOL-KIT

- Gratitude can bridge us from negative emotional states to positive.
- We are responsible for creating a spirit of gratitude.
- When we are in gratitude the smallest things can become the biggest things.
- Gratitude creates a positive mental framework, and from this perspective, negative events and circumstances lose their power.
- Taking a daily gratitude inventory is an excellent way to activate the spirit of abundance.
- Giving and sharing are the natural emotional expressions of gratitude.

The Language of Gratitude

"I am in appreciation for everything I have, and it is enough."

CHAPTER 18

LIVING FROM THE STILL POINT

"When you're inspired, you activate dormant forces, and the abundance you seek in any form comes streaming into your life." - Wayne Dyer

Hello World

The world can easily appear to be spinning and spiraling out of control. Every day, we pull up the internet or turn on our televisions and are bombarded with stories that may negatively affect us. How we view those stories influences our responses. Consider the old woman who lives alone, turns on the news every day, and creates for herself, emotional chaos and turmoil. Whether her day is good or bad is determined by circumstances outside of her control and so, she is emotionally dependent. She's not wrong for lacking self-mastery, because this isn't a case of right or wrong. Her inner turmoil is simply the by-product of being unable to handle events and circumstances that come her way.

Then there's Cameron, a 30-year-old sitting at home, working on his computer. Events and circumstances are happening all around the world, but he shrugs his shoulders, releasing the negative energy. Cameron opens the window and breathes in the fresh air and acknowledges the good in his life. He smiles, knowing that he's been given another day to make a difference. Cameron's commitment to living from his Still Point and spreading love demands his self-reliance.

We are consistently influenced by the media with all kinds of ideas about what's "right," what's "wrong," and what's "offensive." These distractions sideline the real issues needing to be addressed, such as, "how can I be responsible for myself?" Until we can grab hold of the fact that we are responsible for our well-being, we will always look to someone or something else for a solution.

Being home to ourselves and communicating our truths is necessary to generate a positive and far-reaching impact in the world. At the same time, our happiness need not be contingent upon the outcomes we get because that diminishes our personal power.

The fewer requirements we demand of others, the more self-reliant we become. Emotional self-reliance is when we don't expect anyone else to take care of us and realize that is our job.

Tapping into self-mastery means that we shift the focus toward self-reliance rather than dependence. It's about believing in possibilities about which we may not even be aware. Emotionally self-reliant people understand that we'll be fine, and the Universe will provide, regardless of the circumstances.

The opposite of this is dependence, which leads to a mindset of deprivation. From this position, there is a perceived scarcity of everything, including love. This activates fear consciousness in which we choose actions that cause us pain. Being self-reliant or dependent is learned from our families, friends, and society. If we haven't emotionally matured, it's our responsibility to self-educate. The good news is that it can be learned and applied to transform our lives.

Today, our feelings are put through a plethora of ups and downs, delivered in a variety of ways. Often, we receive instincts and impressions through social media channels. These might immediately cause us to react with highly charged responses. This likely prompts us into a conversation with ourselves regarding what needs to happen to feel secure. What action does a person need to take? What comment do I need to hear from someone else to feel better? There are tweets and re-tweets all day long such as, "we need this or that to happen."

We are led by media content from one knee-jerk reaction to the next. It's almost as if stories are created out of thin air to keep us enthralled. Previously, there might have been no conversation about an issue and overnight it can become the highest drama. Eyes are wide open around the water cooler when someone is caught on YouTube behaving in a manner that they're not "supposed to." How can we possibly feel peaceful, which is a by-product of a non-judgmental nature? Emotional mastery means not getting caught up in the rhetoric of mini-dramas because there is no empty void waiting to be filled by breaking news. There is no circumstantial drama awaiting our participation and no anticipatory theatrical communiqué waiting to be unleashed. These feeding frenzies must have no effect on us in order for our conscious awareness to naturally spring forth. We are then capable of living life on our terms, not someone else's.

The Heart of Our Identity

We all want to feel good about ourselves and want our feelings to be considered. We want to know that we are loved and appreciated. These are universal desires and needs. So, if we know what most people want, why aren't we treating others the way they want to be treated? How we feel about ourselves, plays a large role in how we treat others. Helping another person to see their special and unique nature is an invaluable contribution to their life and it is a gift not to be underestimated.

As we mature, we no longer lean on others, institutions or organizations to define us. In essence, we no longer seek society's approval. In this state, we assume responsibility to get through circumstances and events and make choices that lead us on a path toward peace and happiness. These experiences have the quality of growing deep roots into the ground that cannot be easily shaken. It's not that our emotional triggers completely go away; rather, we know we can handle whatever is happening. We develop a belief in ourselves and can handle our emotions because we're equipped with the necessary tools. Realizing that we have a choice, we step into the role of decision-maker and act in our own best interests.

Benefits of Self-reliance

As we engage in self-reliant behavior with greater frequency, we generate an inner calm. From that Still Point, we experience peace of mind, level-headedness, and the reduction of stress. We can now help spread peace and calm to others so that they too can benefit. We begin to stop looking outside of ourselves for solutions because we realize the answers are within. This establishes a more independent nature and means we are no longer waiting for someone else to tell us we're OK. Our personal power is retained to a greater degree and we stop giving it away so easily. Clearly identifying emotions feeds our confidence in being able to handle them intelligently. We have become conscious, and though emotions happen, we can react to them powerfully. Perhaps the greatest benefit is we can love more purely, without a needy quality. Greater self-love is the by-product of emotional self-reliance.

The Nature of Self-reliance

Self-reliance is achieved when we control our reactions to emotions instead of allowing them to control us. It involves our ability to handle ourselves throughout events or circumstances before they disturb us. It means that we make decisions that are based on emotional intelligence instead of knee-jerk reactions. It is the result of being in contemplation rather than reaction, which leads to a more peaceful reality. Feelings aren't inherently bad, rather they are an indication of how outside events are affecting our insides. What's important is the quality of our response to the stirring.

Being outward focused is an excellent start to move away from self-centeredness. We can move toward concern for a better world, although not everyone has to agree with how that might look. In fact, we're able to disagree on something without expecting others to agree with us. We no longer rely on other people to feel better about ourselves. Outside opinions, actions, and thoughts do not deter from the good feeling we create for ourselves because we don't take things personally. Outer dialogue says more about others than ourselves.

Our happiness is no longer for sale, negotiable, or bartered. Those who are not emotionally self-reliant, are always waiting for someone else to tell them they're alright. In this scenario, others are always responsible for their well-being. Most often, we are setting ourselves up for disappointment when not experiencing self-reliance.

The Importance of Self-reliance

Because we can't always count on others to make us feel good or happy, we must learn to rely on ourselves. We must begin to develop an inner-trust that enhances our sense of security. This has a calming effect and results in better relationships because we're not making other people our life-support system. It's empowering to know that we are responsible for our lives. If we don't like something, we can change it. We are more available to others and have fewer struggles to confront. People get more of us and we're more able to be present to what's happening. Emotional self-reliance engenders optimism vs. being collectors of pessimism. We are now prepared to take an active role in the world.

TOOL-KIT

• The more we take charge of our emotions, the more we take charge of our lives.
• Relationships are the best opportunity to work on ourselves and issues.
• What we've been told about ourselves, and allowed ourselves to believe can be changed
• As we help ourselves, we are more capable of helping others in a healthy manner.

Language of Inner Stillness

"My inner calm creates limitless opportunity."

CONCLUSION

"Each one has to find his peace from within. And peace to be real must be unaffected by outside circumstances."
- Mahatma Gandhi

Being caught in the quagmire of assessing success based on purely external measures is a short-coming. This is supported by stories of wealthy and famous people who experience incredible emotional pain and use coping strategies to manage their discomfort. A more accurate indicator of success today, is the degree of inner peace exhibited in our lives. Can we master ourselves to the degree that we make intelligent choices, which deliver the greatest happiness? Or are we forever destined to make poor choices and be led by knee-jerk reactions that don't serve our betterment?

How we answer these questions gives us a clue into our inner sanctum of stillness. Being self-reliant and secure, we can participate in the world differently. No longer are we interested in identifying with a victim mentality. We are free to spread our wings and create a life we've only imagined. The power of creation is married to commitment and we must always ask ourselves, "to what am I truly committed?" The answer to that question will be evidenced by the actions we take and the direction we walk.

Events and situations are neutral, but our thoughts about them are not. The awareness of what's going on inside our heads determines the actions we'll take. We alone make meaning of events and circumstances. That meaning determines the quality of our experience, so we are always in control of what we feel and how we react.

Our Still Point runs deep, and beliefs play an important role in achieving a happy life. They merge with our world view, attract events, and create the context for our emotional responses. Our Still Point is directly affected by those beliefs we select to embrace. It is our responsibility to choose wisely, rather than from impulse, to deliver serenity.

Becoming conscious of our actions, thoughts and beliefs means we can assume responsibility for our reality. Since we interpret relationships and events through our world views and assign meaning to them, we create our life experiences in each moment. This diminishes the aspects of blame, judgment and control, because there is no one else responsible for what we are experiencing.

We can tap into aspects of love, such as gratitude, forgiveness, acceptance, letting go and empowering beliefs. So, not only do we attract events, but we create the qualities of our lives - be they positive or negative. In this manner, inner peace itself, is created. Emotional mastery arises when fear is absent. We are free to choose what tomorrow will look like by leaning into our Still Point of inner peace, which is profoundly aware and nonjudgmental.

A strong inner foundation sets us up for successful lives, void of drama, striving, longing and competition. The race is over because it never was about anyone else; it was always about our relationship to our true nature.

Unburdened by traditional views of success, we can fly free, with a resurgent spirit of peace. Success itself has been achieved when we live life on our terms. Redefining it liberates us from a pleasure/pain paradigm and thrusts us into emotional self-mastery.

Doubtless, we've had some powerful conditioning throughout our lives by peers, institutions and organizations. Today, we can choose to take a new direction. The decisions we make fuel our destiny and either connect us to a power in the Universe or deplete us and leave us empty. Ultimately, the choice is ours. Although it is often difficult parting with old ways of being, we discover not only does happiness live on the other side, so does inner peace.

188

ACKNOWLEDGMENTS

We gratefully acknowledge the time and effort of all those who have made this book possible. Aside from the obvious cast of characters such as mothers, teachers, mentors and wisdom keepers, we'd like to give thanks to the following people who made an extraordinary effort to ensure this book would come to fruition.

A special thanks to:

Anthony Kenealy
Audrey Rider
Bobby Chandiramani
Dominic Zaidan
Emily Rouanet
George Carneal
Hayden Harrington
Kathy McCarthy
Matthew Bravo
Meghan Schmidt
Ryan Bent

Made in the USA
Columbia, SC
01 October 2018